M000304522

Seed Thoughts

By
Al Miner & Lama Sing

CoCreations Publishing

Seed Thoughts

Cover art and book design by Susan M. Miner

ISBN- 978-0-9828786-4-4

1. Lama Sing 2. Psychics 3. Trance Channel
I. Miner, Al   II. Title

Library of Congress Control Number: 2012955602

Printed in the United States of America

Editor's Notes

✧ Regarding the summary on the bottom of each page:
Literary license was taken by Al Miner in some cases to summarize a main point in the message into two lines.

✧ Regarding the use of the terms *Christ* and *Master:*
"Jesus is the Way, the example, the blessing. The Christ is the eternal nature of God expressed in His children.
"There is but one. If you bring to us in future a variety of different names, we will answer the same. Those who would not be willing to accept will be honored here, for their intent is of righteousness unto what they believe. So, then, we ask in humbleness that they would respect here in the same way.
"The Christ is a Principle. It is a spirit. It is the life. The Master has brought this Christ consciousness into oneness with Himself and, thus, He has become the Christ, and is *the* Christ. See? Just so many stumble over this." –Lama Sing

✧ Regarding the use of thee/thou/thine:
In the early years of the readings, thee/thine/thou was used nearly exclusively. Over the years, the syntax has modernized, though it can yet be found in the current readings. An interesting side note – As more than one of the Lama Sing group contributes to what is given, sometimes, even within the same sentence and even in current times, thee or thine is combined with you and your, one entity communicating in one form, another communicating in the other.

January 1

In the year 2013 many new hopes will be born into the Earth.

There will come that call to renew and re-center, and the endurance of what has been as the established way of life will flourish again when those who are His claim this.

Strengthen your spirit and brighten the beauty that is your uniqueness as a child of God. As you do this, there will be the opportunity for the Light, and the hope will be as it has been 2000 years ago.

So, we say to you all:

Here is God's peace and love for you ... your Father, whose love never ceases.

Strengthen your spirit and brighten the beauty that is your uniqueness as a child of God.

January 2

You stand at the threshold of a new year. What sweetness and hope shall you place within it?

The bread of life is that which nourishes your spirit. Seek ever to partake of it as it is offered and, as you take this, see it, feel it, know that it grows within you so that you can give that which is beyond the need of self to others who are enhungered. Then, as you give to them, more will be given that you can give yet more.

Look within often now, more and more, as you journey forth into this new year, and celebrate and bring forth the shining light of hope and peace.

Be ready to receive it. Be ready to share it.

For in this, which is now before you, is the calling: It is that which seeks to unify those who are His into a oneness.

Bring forth the shining light of hope and peace. Be ready to receive it. Be ready to share it.

January 3

Let not the ripples of illusion inundate you as their precedence goes before the great change. It is most often in this manner that there are those efforts on the part of what could be called the status quo to resist change.

It would be no different than attempting to tell a mighty oak tree to hold onto its leaves through the coming winter season. It is not created to do that. Neither are you, each of you, created to hold onto the past in a manner that limits the future and it is, as with the oak tree, that some of the past events, habits, memories, and so forth must be released to their source, where they can be reborn anew.

You stand before a time of calling that from within. Do this with a joyful heart. Be brave. Step forward. And reach into the seeming unknown that is immediately before you, and you will gladdened of heart and mind when you realize the great gifts of joy and wonder that await you.

Some of the past events, habits, memories must be released to their source, where they can be reborn anew.

January 4

If you seek to know of your purpose, then, begin by seeking to know yourself, for, you are the instrument through which the purpose shall be fulfilled. Claim that instrument with the authority of a child of God who is not challenging but is celebrating that, who is calling out in silent wonder and love, that those who have ears to hear or needs to be fulfilled can join in with you and partake of these, from you and with you.

Let not one day pass you by without affirming these things, without building the potential for your own belief. Build it. Claim it. Live it.

Let not one day pass you by without affirming, without building the potential for your own belief.

January 5

Wheresoever one might find themselves in the passage of an Earth day it is always good to bear forth in front of all else the knowledge that thou art a child of God and, in so doing, to recognize that this is not an idle statement. That the beauty of proclaiming this and feeling it is passing all throughout thy being on all levels. This provides the greater beauty and joy that will come thereafter.

Oft remember, then, to pause to re-invoke this, and re-awaken this awareness as a light that goes before one who journeys in darkness.

Bear forth in front of all else the knowledge that thou art a child of God

January 6

There is within each entity that place of sacredness. The regard that you have for this sacredness gives you power.

There is within each entity that place of sacredness.

January 7

There are those preserving and watching over the Hall of Records and other repositories placed into repositories in the Earth and inter-dimensionally in the Earth, awaiting the appropriate time for the Sons and Daughters of the One God to emerge in consciousness again, whereupon these might be reclaimed for the purposes of good works.

These tools will be, as well, the invaluable knowledge with which to restore the pristine and native beauty of the Earth, that it might become, as such, a garden and endure for an thousand years, more or less, and possibly beyond.

The Hall of Records will be invaluable tools to restore Earth's beauty, that it might become a garden for an thousand years.

January 8

Those who choose, or those who are willing to become a part of the balancing of all of existence in Earth, will be a part of that which is to come. This is written in the holy works.

Thus, it is as the Master enters again, that those who are His will walk with Him and, in one form or another, do varying works. We cannot give the exactness of this except to say that it is so. And perhaps what shall follow will be as prophesied: the thousand years of peace.

As the Master enters again, those who are His will walk with Him and, in one form or another, do varying works.

January 9

The very first fingers of light of the entrance of that which is the expectation, the Promise that was given so many Earth years in past and has been given so oft in so many places, is now before those who are seeking. This is that time upon the Earth that has been sought.

Now is the time for the application and the living of that which has been gained through the teachings, through the searching. Bring this to the forefront and make self ready that, as the pathway is open and the Consciousness begins to enter, that thou art at the ready to receive same.

Now is the time for the living of that which has been gained through the teachings, through the searching.

January 10

Free yourselves. You do this by releasing the past and the emotional bond that that holds upon you. You are not responsible for what has gone before, in the sense that so many of you imagine it. But if you cling to it, if you claim it, then you are responsible for that.

Releasing and blessing is often the greatest gift that one can give, even in the face of that which seems mandatory that you be present and that you do this or that thing. Sometimes illusions are very powerful, but Truth is greater.

Look for the truth within yourself, and let it shine, dissipating the shadows of illusion, of self-judgment, of fear, remorse, and all that sort.

Why not, right now, state to yourself, "I am incarnating now into the Earth into a new lifetime. What has gone before is interesting, curious, sometimes humorous, sometimes not so much so. But that's all it is. Just the past."

Releasing and blessing is often the greatest gift that one can give.

January 11

Call forth, ever, dear friends, that which is within you that seeks to be born. Call forth that which is of light and hope.

Call forth that which is within you that seeks to be born.

January 12

An adept is an entity who has begun the practice of, his true and complete nature. An adept may be recognized by some or by none, dependent upon the will of that entity, and can walk in the pathway of the average entity, but it would be the work that would be important to the adept that would have caused them to choose that way of life. They would not be bound, but they would be present, using a spiritual strength to overcome any present limitation, and using their physical presence to be encouraging and supportive where opportunity presented itself. The adept has no true purpose in remaining in Earth except that the knowledge of the adept is such that to remain therein is to remain in service ... soul work or soul purpose unto which they are committed. The adept is never alone in the sense of companionship and more oft than not has knowledge of that presence.

The adept becomes a master when there is the transition of all those limitations and the knowledge which was sought after becomes expressed and, thus, is as wisdom and liberates the entity from the final illusions.

The adept becomes a master when wisdom liberates the entity from the final illusions.

January 13

When traveling and in crowds or dense population areas work on being joyful. Joy has one of the most powerful field generator potentials of all the emotional energies. An attitude of personal inner joy and peace can transcend dis-ease and errant energies as a warm knife through butter, as you call it in the Earth. There is no energy that can counteract it, for, errant energy does not possess, generally speaking, joy.

When you pack your things to take a journey, or you climb in your transport to go to another place, also pack and put in that transport a large helping of joyful energy. Affirm it over and over again. Laugh aloud. Smile. These powerful generative, healing forces within you can protect and preserve you beyond your comprehension.

An attitude of inner joy and peace can transcend dis-ease and errant energies as a warm knife through butter

January 14

There are, of course, many different forms of service and, from the Earth, as a realm of consciousness, service takes on many factors, in terms of its interpretation and application. There are those factors that are derived from the conditioning from birth onward through the family, and interaction with friends and colleagues and such, and those factors that come into play that are of the eternal nature of thine own soul.

And so is it good for all to look upon, "How shall I serve? First, that I shall fill mine own cup and, second, that I shall, from the overflowing of this within me, offer this unto all whom I meet and with whom I interact."

The blessings of the Father cannot be eliminated, blocked, forestalled, plugged up or any such as might be used as a descriptive term here. But they can be ignored. Look you, then, deep within thine own being and find the blessings of our Father there, always waiting for you to reach within and bring these forth. If you seek to serve, do so from the fullness of being a child of God.

If you seek to serve, do so from the fullness of being a child of God.

January 15

Do note, as has been given in past through numerous good workers, Spirit is the pattern from which the greater strength can be drawn. Thus, supplement the spiritual as you do the body. Exercise both vigorously and with dedication each and every day.

Supplement the spiritual as you do the body. Exercise both vigorously and with dedication each and every day.

January 16

There is never a step that you take wherein you are alone. When you stumble and fall, there are many who rush to pick you up. It is considered, here, a great blessing, an honor, a joy, to be among those who actually do the lifting. If you have a sorrow in the Earth, many here rush to be with you to share it. You see, they do not differentiate between joy and sorrow. They see both to be merely experiences, those which do not endure ... only your response to them, only your reaction and what you hold and carry forth from them.

Love the worst within you and celebrate the best. If you see and adjudge yourself as having fallen or taken a misstep upon the pathway you've chosen, can you rush to pick yourself up and love yourself, and forgive, and celebrate the joy of the opportunity that is now ahead?

Love the worst within you and celebrate the best.

January 17

When a soul transcends the veil of separateness from Earth into realms beyond, the incredible wonder and glory of the majesty of creation itself is felt in every aspect far beyond that of the sensory mechanisms known to you in Earth.

They are met by those who carry the brightest of all lights who are believed upon and trusted, loved, prayed to.

And they are embraced in an attitude of love and compassion, unbounded, undefined, and so far beyond the comprehension of a temple of flesh that, here again, words cannot connote the majesty and wonder of their experiences.

When a soul transcends from Earth into realms beyond
words cannot connote the wonder of their experiences.

January 18

Looking into darkness and seeing naught because there is no light, or looking into the light and seeing nothing because there is no darkness to give the gradient of form ... These are one and the same. The exception, here, would be in your understanding.

The Light goeth forth as the *Word* of Father, and the Darkness is that which is the eternal *Presence* of Father. Dwell on this, and you will find your answers.

The Light goeth forth as the *Word* of Father, and the Darkness is that which is the eternal *Presence* of Father.

January 19

Beyond the twilight of what lies ahead shall come a Call. Open your hearts, open your spirits, to hear these words of truth: the Call will be given seven times.

Let your spirits remember this moment, for they shall be as seven golden steps that each of us shall reclaim the beauty, the wonder, the preciousness, of the gift we bear.

The Call will be given seven times. Let your spirits remember

January 20

Remember, you have the power through your intent, through your prayer and, by the nature of your spirit, to contribute to the balancing of any energies, whether that is in the body of one entity or the Earth body, itself.

Thus, these are good times to continually remember that meditation is not just a time of rest. It is not just an experience wherein you call out to God, hoping to hear a response. Meditation is also exercise to the soul, to the spirit of Self.

You have the power to contribute to the balancing of any Energies.

January 21

In the process of attuning self, there is the action of aligning the body according to its energy centers, which, in turn, impact the seven major glandular centers and the subcenters of the body and stimulate the entirety of the neurological system, as well.

Do these things often:

Meditate.

Look for, identify, claim and live your ideal, purpose and goal.

Look at self with loving honesty. Do not deny that which limits you, but know it, claim it, and empower yourself, thereby, to change it.

Do not deny that which limits you, but know it, claim it, and empower yourself, thereby, to change it.

January 22

When you arise on the morn, look within and see the Light before you greet the day and give thanks to the beauty our Father has placed there. And promise yourself that you will be true to this, that you will honor this beauty of your uniqueness. Then, when you open your eyes and look to the dawning, you will recognize the Light as that which is within. You will recognize It as Father smiling back upon you.

Pause here and there as it is joyful for you, not as a mandate, or as a rote or dogma that binds, but as that which is the glorious opportunity to give again and again in prayer.

And, as the sun recedes below the horizon again for that day, look to the Light within once more and, as you see the sun's last rays settling upon the land about you, send your Light with the sun as it journeys around and about to bring its gift of light and warmth to others of your brethren, known and unknown. Celebrate the completion of this day's journey and look to yourself for the goodness of it. And look at others, as they have touched your day's journey, and give thanks for them and bless them, as they are blessing you.

Each day is a holy ceremony of life and you are the one giving the prayers in that holy ceremony. You are the one empowered to give the blessings, to give the sacraments of joy and peace to all.

Each day is a holy ceremony of life. You are the one empowered to give the sacraments of joy and peace to all.

January 23

Water is the symbol of spirit. It is the symbol of God. If one is at one with his Father, would they not, first and above all, find total harmony with water? Water is present both symbolically and literally in nearly all things in the Earth ... indeed (we are advised), in all things to one extent or another. So, if one is at harmony, in a state of oneness, with water, that is Spirit, are they not to the greater or lesser degree instantly in harmony with all things? If thee command an entity to be healed in the name of the Christ, dost thou not speak to their spirit? Dost thou not speak to their waters of life?

In each lesson given by a master there is a certain symbol, some certain phrases which can be used as keys to sustain a consciousness and to retain and be able to quickly apply a truth or a law. If thee seek, then, to command and be at one with the forces of thy sphere, think thou of water. If thee seek, then, to be in harmony with all things and to give life and love unto them, think thou of water.

Ponder in thy secret place these words, for they are words of truth, and we give them unto thee now that they shall set thee free.

If thee seek, then, to be in harmony with all things and to give life and love unto them, think thou of water.

January 24

Our Father who art in heaven... Consider that. Heaven, being thought of in one sense as being the purest and highest state of existence; also being thought of as the purest and best as you are capable of forming in your thought, so, you are saying, *All that is powerful in the highest that I can construe, that I can conceive, the greatest and best within me.* For, surely, if the Father liveth, He liveth within thee. Then, is this not, as well, *God within me, God in my highest place, that which is best within me?* So, you are summoning the highest from within.

If you live in an attitude that affirms that God is within and that this is the highest and best, then, you will begin to transform your life. You will begin to emanate this aspect, this quality of existence, that it shall first precede you and penetrate all that is your experience ... perhaps the most powerful and most blessed affirmation that might be used in any prayer.

Live in an attitude that affirms that God is within and that this is the highest and best.

As one believes themselves to be, along with their brethren, children of God, how can it be that there should come after all this any thought that mankind is powerless, helpless, merely flotsam and jetsam upon the forces that prevail? Shall it be the sea, then, that will vanquish the sons and daughters of God? Can they not call upon the sea as the Master has demonstrated it?

To be sure, there are those who will not hear and cannot see and, for these, their time may be to enter into a new way of life to learn, to grow, and to understand. As the changing of seasons and the great trees of the forest shedding this season's leaves, just as easily so might these who cannot hear nor see begin a new season, and shed the leaves of this life. But this should not be with an eye towards fear or panic. It should be with loving understanding, that those who will are called and those who are willing to give shall receive.

Those who will are called and those who are willing to give shall receive.

January 26

So, as it is written, He shall appear and, perhaps, thee might be called unto His service, but this we know from the information before us: All whom can unburden themselves can enter therein to the next Salem (or Jerusalem, as it has come to be later called). If you see the Light open, and One comes to emerge forth from same, how shall you answer yourself within?

These things, then, we encourage you to consider. If you adjudge a past action from self or another and know it not to be good, is it better that you shall mourn for the rest of the days the commission of that action, or to look to this day as an opportunity to replace thoughts of darkness with hopes of light?

The eternal Teacher of Righteousness shall return. In order to be called, you must forgive just as quickly and as easily as you would be forgiven. Once having attained this attitude, you can become the joyous expression that shall mark you with His own mark, that ye would be called one of His own flock. See?

Look to this day as an opportunity to replace thoughts of darkness with hopes of light.

January 27

Many are called, but in past few have answered. Would ye answer now, in this time? When have you last been in joyous prayer for another soul? Today? This Earth week? Perhaps, last month?

Do you not know that a prayer given to another, openly and lovingly, returns you ten prayers from the Master? From the forces aligned with the Christ? There is not a soul among you who is not worthy to be at the side of the Christ. If you do not believe this, then you are in darkness. Believe it. Know it. Live it.

In the power that you have within you lies the hope and future of your realm.

A prayer given to another, openly and lovingly, returns you ten prayers from the Master

January 28

We offer this message from the Master:
Do remember, in your prayers and meditations, to surround the children with your love and the Father's peace. Do this in my Name.

Remember to surround the children with your love and Father's peace. Do this in my Name.

January 29

The guidance is to know that God is that very force of life which enables your body to exist in your plane and, as you will recognize this to be God, at least your closest perspective of His Being, all things are possible unto you. All joys and happiness, even beyond as ye can conceive, are yours to claim.

But, if ye create an idol, a monument of worship apart from this Force of Life, which is you, then you have created a separateness from that which is the Source of all things.

All wisdom, all power, all joy, love, compassion, all of these aspects and more than thee can describe are a step apart from you.

All things are possible unto you, and all joys and happiness, even so beyond as ye can conceive.

January 30

We have given here oft that there are, in the consciousness, many different expressions of the Christ and that this
spirit is universal, not singular, not held within the walls of
any temple, chapel, synagogue, church, or what have you that
it might be called ... not the veils of separateness but, rather,
that one and all would see the goodness in all, the presence
of God as a Light seeking to shine brightly from each teaching, each man or woman of wisdom.

Then what to do? Only this: Turn about and look to another as they hold their truth and accept this just in the same
manner, and turn to find another, and another, and on and
on. For, the truth of God lies within each of you, dear friends.

There are, in the consciousness, many different expressions
of the Christ and this spirit is universal, not singular.

January 31

Until one has experienced the full measure of their own finiteness it is often not possible for them to grasp and truly accept their infiniteness. In other words, by reaching your current state of "rock bottom" you are much more motivated, much more inspired, to reach beyond yourself for the solutions, the answers, and the methodologies which can enable you to experience joy in your current life.

That, you see, is the primary intent of all souls' progressions and experiencing. For, within each experience, there is intended to be a procession of opportunities which lead to the rediscovery of the true potential of self. From within this potential, then, there is understood that being at one with God is to be in a complete state of joy, for, nothing is seen as loss or limitation. It is seen in its true state: as merely a projection of opportunity for growth and understanding.

Until one has experienced their own finiteness it is often not possible for them to grasp and truly accept their infiniteness.

February 1

Denial ... When an entity in the Earth denies their one-ness with God they become limited.

When an entity denies themselves the joy of living life with all of the senses as bright and brilliant and receptive as possible they become limited.

When an entity refuses to care for their body, even though they might know that such needs are important, they are denying their body.

When an entity withholds love and compassion and kindness, generosity, patience, and all the virtuous words and terms and such that you can muster, they are denying them, as well, from themselves.

When an entity in the Earth denies their oneness with God they become limited.

February 2

Do develop in the forthright attitude that future activities will become much more hectic, much more active in days just ahead, especially so as the Master's Spirit enters the Earth plane with greater and greater intensity.

Find the need for quiet places and places of tranquility, away from the mass-mind thought where God's creations are still intact.

Do take self away from mass-mind thought occasionally, wherein you can commune with the greater spirit that surrounds and is abundant in those areas less dense or less populated by mass-thought of mankind. Every entity on the Earth plane should be aware of the need for this during these times in Earth history, for, the clarity of mind will be prized far above all during days to come.

Take self to quiet places and places of tranquility occasionally, where God's creations are still intact.

February 3

If one is lamenting their lot in life, if one is constantly in need, then that is their lot ... lamenting and need.

Remember the analogy regarding the good farmer who sows his seeds with expectations and hopefulness, whose intention is to tithe a portion to those who serve, to those who bring blessings and joy to him and his family? Do you tithe to yourself? If you are lamenting and holding all the collage of negative emotions and thoughts that you can subscribe to, need we question which seeds you are sowing in the garden of your own life? Cast them out, and claim the good seeds offered to you constantly by the Christ, by the Master, right now, even as we speak.

It is your heart that is the altar, the temple, of your own worthiness, and it is that selfsame altar of worthiness in which the Light of God can shine forth. Fear, a sense of impending loss, a feeling of personal failure, grief, self-judgment of limiting proportion, feelings of sadness and remorse which are based upon the past: What do these contribute? What are the fruits of so doing?

Do you tithe to yourself? Your heart is the temple, of your own worthiness in which the Light of God can shine forth.

February 4

The temple of God is eternally within you. You are the unique one sent to the Earth to bring it flowers, to bring it hope. So, now your call for assistance has been answered. Not we, for we are the humble servants of God, but God has answered you. Don't you know it? Don't you feel it?

Lift that hope up. Embrace it. Pause every morning to say thank You, Father, and then go forth into the day giving those thanks, that gratitude, to all whom you meet.

You are the unique one sent to the Earth to bring it flowers, to bring it hope.

February 5

There is the mantle of truth that comes from above and from beyond that sayeth unto you, "These are times of change, sweet child of God. Be thou of stout heart and spirit." As you can give it, give it, but do not lament. For, the greater cometh, and those times which are of peace and joy shall come and embrace you and lift you up.

Therefore, as you have that which can be given to meet the thirst of that which is in need, give it, whether it be a plant or a tree in your garden, or another you meet who is need and who thirsts for the truth of spirit.

These are those times as have been foretold long ago and recently. Know this, then: The peace of God cometh and settles upon the hearts and minds of those who are seeking and asking and opening themselves to be one with Him.

The peace of God cometh and settles upon the hearts of those seeking and opening themselves to be one with Him.

February 6

This is good for all: that one sees self and knows self and knows one's own thinking, one's own joys, one's own sorrows, the fears and the faith.

These things, see, are the building blocks. These set the patterns that are, generally speaking, percolated, precipitated, if you will. But they are absorbed into the mind as a way of thinking, and stimulate the body just as obviously as an electrical current would stimulate a physical form.

Joys, sorrows, fears and faith ... These are the building blocks. These set the patterns.

February 7

It is good for all to consider within themselves during these times of balance, "What is my nature? Is it unto that which I find present in the daily influences borne unto me by the mechanisms of Earth, or does it flow from something within me, not so much defined in terms of the material but moreso as an ideal that springs forth joy from my heart as I contemplate it?"

Then, think on these things and know them. For, in the knowing of them can you claim power – dominion, you see – with and over them. It is not to suggest that this is good and that is bad, only that you should look within self to see, Is this contributing to my journey or is it added baggage as I travel?

What is my nature and where is my direction? Does it flow from an ideal that springs forth joy from my heart?

February 8

It is good also to consider, "What is my source of joy?"
First and foremost, "Do I *have* a source of joy?"
As odd as that might sound, many of you may find, at first
glance, that you cannot identify a single source of joy. You
might offer an array of things, but no sense of a direction
which brings joy in the doing, in the being, as in daily life.
These things we offer to you as gifts, guidance, if you will,
not mandates. For, the greatest of all guidance always comes
from within you, for, therein, is that temple in which the
Spirit of God is always awaiting you.

The greatest of all guidance always comes from within you.
Therein, the Spirit of God is always awaiting you.

February 9

Any activity performed on one end of the neurological system correspondingly triggers another sympathetic reaction on the other. And, so, the massage to the toes and soles of feet, creates a sympathetic reaction cranially, producing a state of ease by the production of enzymes or endorphins as categorically defined in the Earth. These, then, tend to purify by enervating or effacing ... by that, we mean displacing or reducing the quantity of errant energies and drosses which are stimulants errantly to the glandular and to the neurological system.

Another method here would be to obtain something like a canine toy, rubber, with nubbins on them, bumps or protrusions, and roll this about on the toes and soles of feet, just as you are seated, relaxing.

The third, which is given last in order here but actually the best, is if someone else could massage them for you, and would do so with a cheerful heart. If they can't, don't ask.

Massage to the toes and soles of feet creates a sympathetic reaction cranially, producing a state of ease.

February 10

Ego, greed, fear, lust, avarice, self-denial, pity, hunger, anger. These are all the parts of the mechanism associated to the mass-mind thought, and contributing at present to the Earth plane.

There is always a balancing force. Among these we find the following: faith, love, prayer, hope, charity, forgiveness, compassion, long-suffering, grace.

Ego, greed, fear, lust, self-denial, pity, hunger, anger are all associated to mass-mind thought contributing at to the Earth.

February 11

Know thyself, and all that you seek and greater will come before you.

It is in the Knowing that you can accomplish your quest to be free.

Know thyself, and all that you seek and greater will come before you.

February 12

How to serve God, you ask? We tell you God is within you, and He is within thy neighbor.

If you wish to serve Him, in truth, you must first serve yourselves. When you step forth this day will you look unto your neighbor in thy old habits and will you greet one along thy way only with a casual glance, not a care for their needs or a kind word for their ears to behold? And, what of thy loved ones? Will you bypass their request for your kindness and attention? Will you even turn away from your own needs?

We submit these comments humbly. They are not intended as criticisms, you see. They are merely factual comments which now need expression. We hope the expression sparks an awareness in each of you, so that you may recognize the search begins within you.

How to serve God, you ask? We tell you God is within you and He is within thy neighbor.

February 13

Your potential is limited by your need because you might need it so badly that you forget how to create. In other words, desire becomes a veil clouding your potential.

When one is in harmony they are unlimited. When one has strong personal needs, those needs can limit. The key to unlimited potential is being unlimited ... that simple. You possess what you are willing to possess freely. If you must possess it, you have built a barrier to allowing it to manifest.

When one is in harmony they are unlimited.

February 14

The attainment of balance ... This is accomplished, first, by seeking within self to know that you are an eternal creation of God. In so doing, the shift to the awareness of a more eternal nature changes the emotive and the finite issues that are involved in same.

Know that you are an eternal creation of God.

February 15

There are those moments in a journey such as life in the Earth wherein one ponders, what are the influences? What are the patterns and forces that have gone before that have predicated a certain condition in the current measure of time?

And, yet, always is there present that Power, which is the oneness of God with each of thee, that can command these forces, just so as the Master, the Christ, has given it.

It is ever important, then, to recognize that even the subtlety of doubt can be a deterrent from claiming such in the fullness of its power.

Nonetheless, claim it! Do what you can and know to do to place your authority and the blessings of the Father's gifts to thee before all the challenges, good or not so good ... with a note of loving humor, for, it is dependent upon the perceiver the measure of that, see.

Do what you know to do to place your authority and the blessings of Father's gifts to thee before all the challenges.

February 16

There is no separateness. All traits, qualities, or what have you, are all one under the title of Our Father. Each bears a separate petal of the lotus, so to say. See?

Be mindful that the journey in Earth is filled with opportunity and these are as opportunities as one would choose to make them. It serves no purpose to look upon another's choice and to determine it good or bad. It simply is their choice.

It is good for all to remember that the choices of others are in accordance with the Father's Will. Therefore, might they not be sacred?

It serves no purpose to look upon another's choice and to determine it good or bad. It simply is their choice.

February 17

Those who choose will be chosen.

Those who choose not will be given that blessing to continue on and choose as they would.

Those who choose will be chosen.

February 18

Believe unto that which is sacred within you, and within you alone. And, if you come together with others who hold a sacredness within themselves that is a reflection of your own, then, your coming together as a group brings forth a strength and a power that is of wondrous potential.

Look within yourselves to bring forth that which is your own truth and that holy uniqueness, that it can be that which is seen and felt by others. This is one of the greatest works that you can do in these current times. And, as you gift this to others who have joined with you, all of you are lifted up beyond the curtains of illusion ... one step, another, and another, and another. And, soon, you will see the freedom of your own beauty coming forth from within.

Look within yourselves to bring forth that which is your own truth and holy uniqueness.

February 19

The attitude of fear creates an imbalance, or is an accelerant to a state of imbalance.

Here's the idea, then: that you would recognize one of the greater remedies for most all things that are amiss is joy and peace. Joy comes from the state of realizing that you are a child of God, and by claiming that and living it and being it; living a state of peace and living the attitude of happiness, an attitude of expectancy, joyfully; and believing in self, not looking to be as another is or many others are, but looking at self as that creation of God which is a treasure to God.

Were it so that God wished to have all perfect in a certain categorical definition, then, it would be so. It is not so. The perfection lies within each individual. When this is seen and claimed, then, the beauty of the concert of God's intent is manifest, and all will benefit from it. Try to forgive. Try to live a life of love, beginning with self and, after that, it will automatically be given to your planet and to all upon it. See?

Try to forgive. Try to live a life of love, beginning with self.

February 20

Understand that that which is taken into the body physical is that, in the sense of the ingredients or substances, of which mind can, for the better, build.

By way of identification, there are numerous food groups, numerous nomenclatures, by which the mind would identify these varying elements or substances which are comprised into the food groupings, and there are varying aspects which can be the differing viewpoints when one is studying same.

We wish to impart this as the general philosophies or concept: That, as one becomes moreso and moreso attuned to the presence of God's guidance within self, then, that of the gentle urging of the body, the mind, and the spirit, can, in its combined form, be that which helps self to identify those foods or food groupings which are for the better ease of the body at this time, in that place, and in accordance to those needs which may be prevalent in same.

As one becomes attuned to God's guidance within self, then, self can identify those foods in accordance to its needs.

February 21

Some may find shadows about the Earth, and they turn to see, "What is this that casts a shadow upon me? My life?" Some may feel or sense an impending fear, a danger, or a disaster. Some may see the New Madrid fault trembling, shuddering. Others may see the Ring of Fire stir, others, quiet summits rumbling into renewed life.

In all of this, steal yourselves in prayer and joyful oneness with God, that you would know that these are those times prophesied, and that you might recall with clarity that our Lord God would ever honor his prophets, those who bear His Word: All that might occur in and about the Earth is only that which is a part of the prophecy and the time of change.

Must it be of great turmoil and disaster? It would not be wrought by God, but wrought by the hearts and minds of the children of God. For, the greatest of all gifts also affords each of them the greatest opportunity. That the gift might be ignored or misused is the right of Free Will.

Thus, look about in gladness for that which shall be and, just as a traveler upon a lengthy journey; keep thine eye upon that which is the destination, the Ideal; and know that each step lifts thee up unto that time when it shall be attained.

Steal yourselves in prayer and joyful oneness with God, that you would know that these are those times prophesied.

February 22

Your meditations should seek to find that state of balance that sees beyond just the events of the day, just the events of the week, month, and year, to see yourself as one who has come to the Earth to journey for a time, and that that time has a portal of departure that the soul can journey on elsewhere.

You are intended to have an experience of peace and joy. Seek ye, then, the inner peace and that which sees all things as they merely are and not that which has triggering points in the emotion, not that which can call to thee and bring forth some past memory or emotion and make it resident within you.

There should be the call always to your own spirit.

Seek to find that state of balance that sees beyond just the events of the day.

February 23

Healing might be better understood if one were to view the entirety of their life experience in the Earth plane as just that—having the purpose of developing an understanding of how to heal self and others.

What forces, then, work to prevent effective healing? Certainly, one can surmise or deduce from that as has been given some of the obvious answers to this: lack of faith, lack of concentrated thought, and lack of action. That these are triggered, in essence, by habit, by karmic influences, by the mass-mind thought, and by influences which are often more subtle but which are cosmic and which are, in terms of group karma, more overriding in a general sense.

One might view the entirety of their life as having the purpose of understanding how to heal self and others.

February 24

It is said that love knows no fear because love is God. Therefore, could fear be considered the absence of God? Not truly, for all things are of God. Fear is the mechanism of contrast. Doubt, frustration, anger, are qualities of such emotion, as is love and fear, that are tools for the growth of self.

Does self wish truly to be one with God? Sufficient so as to release these things which are as familiarities of life in the Earth? Then so be it. Release them. As simple as that. When you encounter them as emotions or events in your life, dear friend, think in that moment that the Master stands at your side. Turn to him, and ask, "Heal this. Help me to understand it that, in so doing, I might release it." Ask Him to take it from thee and return, in its place, understanding, forgiveness, long-suffering, faith, but most of all love.

Does self wish truly to be one with God?

February 25

What do you think is the reality of eternity? It is good to reflect upon this.

If the end of the journey you are upon is to come on the morrow or in a fortnight or in a year, what would be your thoughts, your attitudes, your actions? Some would say they will take all they can while they can. Others will say they will do this or that.

All of these answers have no great meaning, for, the one point is, "I seek to know myself for what I am." The answer to that question is, "I am an eternal child of God."

The Master, called Christ, is your Brother. He is an eternal child of God. Seek ye this, and believe, and it shall become the next destination accomplished.

I am an eternal child of God.

February 26

Remember how very much you are loved. If you can remember Father's love of you and for you, you will be enriched beyond measure.

One way to remember this is to tell Father of your love for Him.

If you can remember Father's love of you and for you, you will be enriched beyond measure.

February 27

In each time of darkness, some truth is present. In each time of light, some darkness is present.

When the dark and light move into a state of harmony you do not have opposing forces perched delicately upon a balance scale. You have opposing forces that can now polarize themselves into a majestic expression of harmony that will possess, as the result, the idiosyncratic uniqueness of all manner of expression.

Where you have had, as you consider analogous to light and darkness, that called black and white, you will in its place now have the entire spectrum or rainbow of potential.

In each time of darkness, some truth is present. In each time of light, some darkness is present.

February 28

Like a child that stirs in its sleep this way and that and, surely, the bedclothes become disarrayed, so is the Earth like that child. It will come to a state of good rest and good being but, for the now, have a faith to know that the greater cometh.

Fear not that which is lost but, rather, ever look to that which lies ahead. These are, indeed, times of change and, as the Earth stirs as that sleeping child, it will cause some disarray. Indeed, some will lament their lack of rain and others will lament their abundance of it. Find peace in either or both or any such action of change, and know that that which comes is greater than the sum of all of these.

Fear not that which is lost but, rather, ever look to that which lies ahead.

March 1

Twisting and bending exercise:

- With the feet about two-thirds a meter apart, firmly placed, standing erect, hands on the hips, body and spinal column erect, looking straight ahead, turn your head to the left. As you do so, allow your right elbow to follow your vision. Turn to the left as far as you can comfortably, and bounce back and forth about eight to ten times to the extent or limit comfortable. Then hold the position extended to the left for a count of ten.
- Now go back to center, looking straight ahead, chin up, and now do the same to the right, repeating the bouncing. When you have completed this to the right, come back to the center, looking straight ahead.
- Now, bend forward, keeping the head and spinal straight. Bob up and down, just a bit, and then stand erect.

Do not overexert, but to the limit. Each day this will progress. Repeat this two, three times in succession, three to five times daily for the first two weeks, two or three times for the next two weeks, and twice daily thereafter.

What will this do for you? Just about everything. It will flex the Leydig and the spinal and align the glandular, stimulate the lymphatics and re-distribute them, aid in the re-balancing of the alimentary, increase the sense of balance in the physiological sense, stimulate the neurological system, and on and on. ... simple and of great meaning to you.

The twisting and bending exercise twice daily ... What will this do for you? Just about everything.

March 2

Look for those whose light is dim and, though ye need not do a thing, seek briefly that place within. And, from your spirit, give unto them and, from the eye or from the heart, send it. In this manner, so does the Master yet do these same works.

For, it is written that the spirit remembers the mind and the heart of the flesh. The temple of flesh endureth only as it endures in the medium of life, itself, in the Earth; but the spirit remembers and holds any light it has been given, and will take same into the afterlife and will find greater blessing upon their transition from such an offering.

It is such a simple, little work, so it would seem ... the thought sent to one in need, the prayer offered without request, the extended hand in spirit to lift up a wearied spirit that one might encounter.

The spirit remembers and holds any light it has been given, and will take same into the afterlife

March 3

Many refer to the Revelations in conjunction with the current time. Unto such people we state an affirmation, for, as are called the Four Horsemen, these are visible in and about the Earth even as we speak, and they feed upon the ignorance, the hatred, the hostility, and the ego of each soul. If ye would stop dis-ease, pestilence, then begin by the conclusion of your own nourishment of them. Do not adopt an attitude of guilt regarding this, but lovingly seek in a spirit of truth to know yourself. For, in the discovery and acceptance of what you are comes the first step in becoming what you would like to be … that of your highest ideal.

Preservation of material things shall indeed become difficult in the years ahead. Shifts in power, in authority, and in means of barter and/or exchange are foreseen here as imminent. Value considerations will change. Things which were considered commonplace will become of value, and things which were of value will be of no concern any longer. Truth will be sought in all quarters and the beast shall turn upon itself. Some seas shall redden with its anger and its fury, and the seat of the European shall change, three times in succession under the admonition of its own denial of its heritage.

In the discovery and acceptance of what you are comes the first step in becoming what you would like to be

62

March 4

Because something is in the past does not mean it is over. It is only over when you release it and go on. If you carry the past with you, then, do so joyfully for the good fruits harvested from same.

If you carry the past with you, then, do so joyfully.

March 5

No power is greater than the power you are willing to claim.

No light can ever be any brighter than that light you find in the sanctuary within your own being and which you bring forth.

No wisdom is clearer, sharper, keener than that which you have gained through the journeys of your spirit, the experiences of your current lifetime brought to the altar of truth and honor within, and carefully weighed and measured, that your path becomes guided by this wisdom, and your service, thereafter great.

No song can be sung sweeter than the song of your own heart when it is filled with the joy and resonance of love. For love is the song of God spoken in the Word of God which goes forth from you in your being, in your word, your action and deed. For love is the Light of God, and it penetrates and transcends all illusion, that such be revealed for its own nature and intent.

Love is the Light of God, and it penetrates and transcends all illusion.

March 6

When two or more gather together with like mind and intent, and joyfully perceive, search, and inquire, this broadens the perception and understanding of all involved and, potentially, creates the opportunity for a blessing to be born in the Earth that conceivably could endure evermore.

When you encourage an entity in your daily life, just a smile, a kind word, a compliment, this is the same ... an enduring gift that will surely be remembered and a clear, open, loving line of light. It will subtly connect you to that entity to perpetuate blessings on into what you call the future that might seem inconceivable because of, comparatively speaking from your perspective, the smallness of the act.

Within you is that Light of Father, just the same as when you first awakened.

March 7

Prayer is precious. It is the life-force which thee have. As thee pray, thou art giving thy life-force unto others, but thee know the Law. The Law says, quite clearly: So as ye have sown, so must ye reap, and manyfold over.

So, do, ofttimes, sow prayers.

If ye do not believe this is true, then, give self the opportunity to be blessed by it and hold to a schedule for thirty Earth days of consistent prayer twice daily. If your life has not improved at that time, at the conclusion of the thirtieth Earth day, if some great blessing and some insight or wisdom has not come to thee, return to us, for we would know thee. For we have seen none whom have not gained a great blessing for so doing. See?

As thee pray, thou art giving thy life-force unto others.

March 8

In the midst of that which is called darkness, a very small light can be of brilliance to guide one on their journey. As the Earth moves through varying veils of separateness, that little light within is, ever, the brilliance ... all that is needed for you to find your way.

That little light within is all that is needed for you to find your way.

March 9

It has been given here often, gently, lovingly, and we shall give it as oft as it is requested of us: There are those who go before the Master's light to make the way open and passable. Not to clear debris from a roadway, but to clear doubt, to cast away fear, hatred, anger, animosity; to build temples unto the understanding and uniqueness of each soul, temples not of stone or wood or berm, but temples that stand in the actions of the faithful ... their words, their deeds, and the very spirit that radiates from them that has the power to heal, that has the wisdom to build on good earth the greatest of all temples, the way of life which exemplifies what should be held spiritually in the many temples that now stand upon the Earth.

Some will think in their hearts that the Master will surely appear in this grand temple, or that wondrous cathedral, or over here in this synagogue, or upon this beautiful and ornate chapel. This we know from he who goes before: that shall the Master's foot rest upon the Earth in the form that can be seen by all, once again, it will be in the same manner as it so did in past, that the Earth shall be his temple; and it shall be sanctified in His Father's Name. There is naught that can contain nor limit and, therefore, He would not let it be so. See?

Shall the Master's foot rest upon the Earth in the form that can be seen by all, it will be in the same as it did in past.

March 10

This is a time of great change. The greatest of all change is in opportunity, not in disaster or cataclysmic Earth change, for, the Earth shall continue.

But what of thee? What of thy eternal nature, every one of you? Do you wish to enhance it? To accelerate your growth, your progress, unto that time when ye shall claim your heritage as Sons and Daughters of the Light of God? Then, know this time to be that wherein His Light is, once again, clearly in the Earth. There are teachers of righteousness in the Earth, and they are stirring. They are growing with each Earth day in their willingness to accept the mantle which is offered to them, once again.

Each of you, in your own unique way, is similarly offered such a mantle, recognition by the Forces of Light.

Each of you, in your own unique way, is offered a mantle, recognition by the Forces of Light.

March 11

Limitation is moreso that image of habitual thinking, of rote, of dogma, than it is reality. More entities dwell in self-imposed imprisonment in their lives in the Earth and other realms than shall ever be physically imprisoned in all of the times and half-times of existence.

If you go into one large metropolis in the Earth at present in your land, you will find so many entities who are veritable prisoners of their habit, of their rote, of their dogma and surprisingly, perhaps, have no idea that they are imprisoned but only bear the end result as a manifestation of this, and that this thrusts itself forward as an expression in their life here and there. Even then, they are willing to forego that potential for joy because they would rather cling to the familiar, to cling to that which is known and, therefore, comfortable, rather than to draw upon the scenario of self-discovery that is required to break oneself free.

Limitation is moreso that image of habitual thinking, of rote, of dogma, than it is reality.

March 12

There is wisdom in realizing that only a certain duration of time should be spent in studying the pebbles that lie at the foot of a great mountain. See? Look at the mountain ... *there* is the great gift and opportunity. The pebbles are just the entrée to it.

The pebbles are the thoughts that can come and go ... the views, the perspectives, and all these things that become a part of the nuances of self, the coloration of who you are. The mountain is the truth of who you are – a great spirit, a potential of a magnitude symbolized by a mountain.

Choose your way by the guidance that cometh from within, for this will always be aright.

Choose your way by the guidance that cometh from within, for this will always be aright.

March 13

So, you see, in each loss ye find gain, and in each gain ye might find some loss.

But can ye not see from the progression of this great and loving Soul the clear demarcation of the way to proceed: using each gain, each loss, as one who balances the scales of justice, a little here, a little there, always seasoned with the willingness to forgive, to cooperate, the diligence of long-suffering and patience?

———————

So, you see, in each loss ye find gain, and in each gain ye might find some loss.

March 14

Within you is that Light of Father, just the same as when you first awakened into your uniqueness. The moreso you cleave unto this light, the greater shall its brilliance reach out to touch all aspects of your being, your consciousness, your actions, words, and deeds. By the claiming, all that is yours awakens in its beauty of uniqueness and its grand opportunity to serve others just so by way of that uniqueness.

―――――――

Within you is that Light of Father, just the same as when you first awakened into your uniqueness.

March 15

If you don't allow yourself to sing and dance – inwardly, see – how can you expect the outer to manifest singing and dancing? Of course, this is metaphorical. Of course, it's allegorical and, of course, it's true.

If you will claim, your lives can be transformed. You have accepted our partnership and we yours. We outnumber you presently thousands to one. We'd be joyful if that ratio would change. We'd be even more joyful of the willingness, complete and total willingness, of those of you who *have* claimed.

Now, that's not to say that we do not see the willingness to varying degrees in all of you, some a lot more than the others, see, because it's difficult, it's awkward ... You could be looked upon as strange in the Earth, blasphemers, demented, on a spiritual wobbly journey, and all that sort.

But some will look upon you and say, "Brother! Sister! I have waited so long for you!"

See?

If you don't allow yourself to sing and dance inwardly, how can you expect the outer to manifest singing and dancing?

March 16

The Earth plane is one of the most sought after realms of expression for souls involved in that level or sphere of consciousness. It is sought after because of the profound opportunity to express and have immediate opportunity to observe and interact with that resulting form, from the expression. So, if you are falling prey to the thought that the Earth plane is a realm, a sphere of Consciousness, which is for less than inspired or illuminated souls (given with a note of loving humor), that is simply not so. It is one of the realms more beautifully in harmony with the creative forces and one of those most profoundly productive in terms of soul growth.

Earth is one of the realms most profoundly productive in terms of soul growth.

March 17

No soul, as we perceive God and creation, is greater or lesser than any other soul. This we have before us in Universal Consciousness. Therefore, we must conclude that, if this is so, all souls are equal, whether angel or that which is called the soul of man, or other such.

If we should find this is not so, then we shall conclude, at that point, all such works, for, we would find there would be no truth in any such that we have done to date or that we might perpetuate, henceforth. We would immediately conclude all works and disband our grouping and depart. For, you see, if there is not truth in this that we have before us, then, we must humbly conclude that truth does not exist.

If there is not equality in our One God, then, what purpose for existence? If there can be a hierarchy, where God would view one greater than the other, we do not believe in this god, and we would depart to seek out what we know there to be as the One True God.

No soul is greater or lesser than any other soul. If there is not equality in our One God, then, what purpose for existence?

March 18

Begin your work upon your belief that you are separate from your Father, for you are not. Understand that you asked to be in the Earth at this time because you knew, when you were here with us, that He would be entering again, and you asked, Lord, let me be there to help prepare the Way. Let me be of service, that we bring good cheer and hope to those who have lost their way or who are dis-eased.

Begin your work upon your belief that you are separate from your Father, for you are not.

March 19

Where you may have had in past two strongly opposing chords of dissimilar vibration, a resplendent chords of harmony can, indeed, be the result. So, as this is manifested, the thought-form follows and, so, as the thought-form follows, the manifestation expands. In turn, a new thought-form emerges because of a new opportunity and, from that, an expansion upon the potential, once again, and this increasing in its frequency and its amplitude and all manner of expression that could convey a wondrous, glorious movement.

Then the foundation is what is important: that you can withstand what you know to be a time of important change; that you can find within you that which is the memory of your perfect nature, your eternal nature, and your heritage with God, who has created the All; and that you learn from discovering this within yourself, that, so as you manifest it outwardly, so will others reflect it back to you and, as they reflect same back to you, it expands again as you, the giver, receive the bounty for having given.

The foundation is what is important, that you can withstand what you know to be a time of important change.

March 20

Just as quickly as a cell can be impacted by dis-ease, equally swiftly can that cell restore itself.

Just as quickly as a cell can be impacted by dis-ease, equally swiftly can that cell restore itself.

March 21

There should always be in each heart and mind that knowledge that your walk upon the Earth plane is for the purpose of learning, gaining, and understanding what it is that the Earth plane, and other planes like this are attempting to bring forth in your consciousness:

There must always be a remembrance that God dwells within and about all things, for, He has created them unto thee and, through thy own hand thou hast, each one, been a co-creator with the Father.

This, each has forgotten, but it shall come unto their minds more and moreso in the days ahead, do you see. Thus, then we suggest: Be that, live that, walk that pathway, then, as the Christ has denoted for you. Not in a ritualistic, self-sacrificing way, but in a joyous, happy, fulfilling attitude, knowing that, in so doing, thou shalt have His love and mercy.

There must always be a remembrance that God dwells within and about all.

80

March 22

There is no error or failure, from the eternal sense, in the progression of a soul or in the experience of a lifetime in the Earth. What there is, is the evolvement of the soul.

In other words, what you consider to be failure is just as important, and ofttimes even moreso, than the accomplishment of that which you call success. For, failure becomes a steppingstone; success, generally, becomes a plateau upon which one tends to arrive into a state of gradual idleness, complacency, contentment and such often does not spawn a continued search or growth-like effort. This is not to imply that one shouldn't strive for success in the true intent of that term, which is to say, a joyful state but, when one measures success by the comparative analyses of the accomplishments or works of others, that measure of success can be illusionary and misleading. For, you are not the others. You are you. You were not created in the sense of being identical to the others in purpose, in potential, in talent, and so forth. You were created individually unique, as you. See? At some point each individual must deviate from the generality, that their own individuality can blossom and come forth in full bloom.

To a large degree, this *is* the wheel of karma: that as each entity recognizes the uniqueness of their own individuality, they come to be more and more gracious, forgiving, understanding, and compassionate about the uniqueness of others.

There is no error or failure. What there is, is the evolvement of the soul.

March 23

Be just a bit more loving and kind to yourselves. Don't be quite so willing to accept the objectives as the physical or material world presents them. Remember to return within often and find your own objectives.

Remember the Master's works. Very often, He would take time apart from all those who cried out in emotion, in anguish, for His presence. He would turn from them to replenish Himself. Only after that time as He knew He was complete and whole and in the best of harmony with God did He return to do those works of our Father. Can thee do less?

Be just a bit more loving and kind to yourselves.

March 24

The changes will be those which will amplify all of the qualities that are within an entity. Thus, if there is a quality which limits, this will become severe. Conversely, if there is a quality which enhances, which enlightens or contributes light and joy to others as well as self, this, too, will be amplified. What shall one do with such changes? Here, then, is the potential as given, called the Glorious Transition:

Those who have consciousness and are seeking will find, and they will find greater than they believe possible. This is that time to keep the watch. This is that time to make manifest that which has been and is your intent in the very action of living life.

Those who continue to live life in a limited form, denying the spiritual and eternal nature of Self, shall meet that end without question. They shall find their return to increase in its limitation. Our prayers are always with these entities, and we encourage you to do the same.

This is that time to make manifest that which has been and is your intent in the very action of living life.

March 25

In the spiritual, all relationships endure throughout eternity, and so we would gently remind you to ever be joyful in the knowledge that when you pass through the far gate of life yourself, you'll be met by these entities joyfully, that is to say, those who have not gone on to take up new experiences (given with a note of loving humor). Even here, you can find their spirit present, even so as you could find their spirit present now or in the future when each is at that stage of readiness for such.

Entities who dwell in the Earth for but weeks or months or a handful of Earth years can easily accomplish some intended work in that time. More often than not, these are benevolent works.

In the spiritual, all relationships endure throughout eternity.

March 26

First, these important steps:

Keeping thy body physical cleansed, healthful and rested, that this is truly a temple wherein the living God can dwell.

Then to the mental body, cleanse those thoughts that are errant in their ways. Search out those mannerisms and those mechanisms which allow thee to be in harmony and in comfort with all those about thee. Strive to find in the recesses or in the corners of your being those thoughts that are harbored in illness towards others. Replace them with the understanding that each entity is a spirit, a part of God, and that without this entity thou would be just a bit less complete.

Within thy body spiritual, an ample and abundant diet of reverent attention. Where is thy meditation during these times? Seek within and find that which is the Eternal Light that will guide thee in each step, each activity. Find reverent periods to commence and to conclude each day's activities. Give thanks for those opportune wherein self is permitted to function and interact in a plane such as the Earth plane. Find for self joy from the interacting of karmic influences, for this is a blessing or pattern which self has woven with others to find for the better understanding and attunement within self.

Finally, be at one with God. That means love thy neighbor unto thyself as an equal, and prove it.

Find reverent periods to commence and to conclude each day's activities.

March 27

When you request or set about a certain goal with an
ideal in your heart, spiritually speaking, you make the way
open and passable for a channel of God's grace and blessings
to flow to and through you. So long as you allow that to flow
through you, you will continue to grow, to gain in your
spiritual illumination, and to be assisted from here and other
realms by those who serve in God's name.

When you set about with an ideal in your heart, you make the
way passable for a channel of God's grace to flow to you.

March 28

As the Master called out to Lazarus and he came forth, so can you call out to self to come forth from the inactivity of whatever is your glory, your potential, your life, which has, in effect, died.

When you succumb to that which is of limitation there is, first, that which looks like slumber and can be more easily awakened and restored. But, as the tenure of that slumber is greater and greater in length and after lifetime upon lifetime so it remains dormant or uncalled, then, it is as a death and you must claim the *I am* within to call it forth.

You can call out to self to come forth from the inactivity of whatever is your glory, your potential.

March 29

Generally speaking, aluminum salts are extremely detrimental to the physical body, largely because of their properties which are such that they remain inert in the body.

It is extremely difficult for the body, if at all possible for some bodies, to cause the particles, the aluminum salt particles, to be dissolved. Anatomically, they are inert. Thus, the types of acidics, which would actually change them in the biochemical or electrochemical sense, are not normally those found in the physical bodies. When such acidics are produced these, can cause byproducts which are damaging to the cells and to the intra-structure of the cell. Largely, the nuclei of the cell becomes deformed, causing errant or migrant cell structure.

Generally speaking, aluminum salts are extremely detrimental to the physical body.

March 30

Your body listens for your words and your thoughts. Your body responds to these. If you laugh, your body laughs. See?

Your body listens for your words and your thoughts.

March 31

The canine is the blessing of God. They have no need for time to balance upon their departure from the Earth plane but, rather, move into the light and warmth and embrace of that such as the mother and the original assembly or litter (we believe you call this) to be embraced and to be held in the warmth and the joy and bounding experiences of oneness.

Thereafter, his energy, his expression follows you. It has followed you in the past and has been with you on several occasions, not always in the canine form, but several times as such, for, that is seen as your favorite. He is with you. He is of spirit. He is as an added energy of blessing about you to bring you love and warmth and simply the caring. The expression of love is returned to you as you have given it.

The wondrous thing about these creatures is that they carry with them love that has been given to them. Whether it be just a bit or a considerable, they carry it with them and they expand this and perpetuate it. As such, this then grows to a point where it can embrace you as another expression of the layers of consciousness or love about you. Very beautiful.

The wondrous thing about canines is that they carry love that has been given to them. They expand this and perpetuate it.

April 1

That which is insoluble can be melted away with the love and laughter of the child within.

That which is insoluble can be melted away with the love and laughter of the child within.

April 2

Now let us speak of this, if we might, for a bit here ... and we do not give this lightly, we give it with the spirit of the Christ before us:

When you depart from the Earth, regardless of the means, what do you anticipate? That you shall know nothing? That you shall simply "not be?" If this is your belief, it will be granted to you until such time as you awaken and call out to God. Then, the pathway that has been followed by many others will be yours, as well.

If you choose to move beyond the Earth but not "release it," then, you will be taken to a place where you will be with others who are of that same belief. There, you can create for yourselves as ye will, and, the greater the number who create of this nature, the greater in significance shall the thought-form become until such time as there shall be a believed reality of its expression.

If you choose to be free of limitation and any of the other myriad of choices before you, there is no limit. If you choose to be free of limitation and to be in the peace and joy of your true nature, and you will not cling to that which limits, then this shall be what you attain.

What determines all of these examples (and they are only a few) is the nature of your spirit, your attitude. If you believe, as given in the humble examples, then, so will it be for you.

When you depart from the Earth, regardless of the means, what do you anticipate?

April 3

There has always been, and there always will be, those blessings upon you from those whom you have served in past. It is ever so for each soul who is in joyful service in God's Name.

It is unto this knowing that we call to you to open yourself to these blessings, that they do not go unreceived, that the glory of these can be felt and known. For, to complete the cycle of service, there must be, you see, the receiving that equals that which has been given. Then can the true beauty and magnificence of each soul rise higher and higher, until all know one another to be their brethren, and love abounds and joy prevails.

There has always been, and there always will be, those blessings upon you from those whom you have served in past.

April 4

He shall return to awaken that which is the Christ within you, each of you, when you have made the way passable for Him.

Then, as the sons and daughters of man shall collectively illuminate the Earth, just so as we here have illuminated the heavens for Him, know that He may again walk from here to thee collectively in the Earth, and that time of Light thereafter shall come to be and sustain itself for many Earth years to follow.

He shall return to awaken that which is the Christ within you, each of you, when you have made the way passable for Him.

April 5

If you are willing and you do that as you know to do, the Kingdom of our Father awaits you, and the glory of our joy upon your entry here shall be no less than the return of the man called Jesus. See?

If you are willing and you do that as you know to do, the Kingdom of our Father awaits you.

April 6

Do not weep over missed opportunity, or you'll only create more of it in the current. See?

Do not weep over missed opportunity, or you'll only create more of it in the current.

April 7

There is that within self which knows of the Word and knows its potential and its great beauty and unlimited power. This consciousness within self also remembers that it is of God, and that this is the Word of God, His will, His power, His grace. This consciousness sees itself in the presence of all other entities and will ever strive to reach out to them, to acknowledge their mutual oneness.

Then, if self reaches that moment wherein the ego, the fears, the doubts, the limitations of that existence can be placed aside for an instant or, through the training or the dedication, such can be made to occur quickly and easily ... In either instance, this entity, this consciousness within self as an entity, rises to the fore and guides with confidence and authority; and the actions which are guided through this inner knowing, this inner consciousness, are those which would lead thee to the Word, to the presence of God. Once this pathway is opened, His Word can flow through thee, just as surely as one who might create a channel for a body of water will find that the water will continue to affect the breadth and depth of its new channel.

———

There is that within self which knows of the Word and knows its potential and its great beauty and unlimited power.

April 8

Truth is the greatest power of all. Why is this? Why would we state this? Because Truth is comprised of all else and thus, the Sacred Truth is the Christ. The Sacred Truth is able to see in truth with clarity, because the sight is made perfect through love and compassion. Because Truth rests upon honor, it rests upon compassion, it rests upon faith, hope, all these things and much more make up what we call Truth.

Then, if thou art true to self, to whom is thy truth given? If you know you are one with God, then, it must follow logically that you are being true to God. If you believe that you can be one with God, then you are permitting God to be one with you.

This is a union that always has been. You are not creating it ... You are claiming it.

If you believe that you can be one with God, then you are permitting God to be one with you.

April 9

This is that time that you, dear brothers and sisters, have sought. He cometh before you. Open yourselves to receive it and it is yours.

Many here of course, are joining with you, reaching out to you, brothers and sisters who have walked with you all throughout this lifetime and with whom you have walked in past, as well. This is the now that has been sought, that has been prophesied. It is the opening of the way.

This is that time that you, dear brothers and sisters, have sought. He cometh before you.

April 10

In this manner will you know Him ...

There will be a gladness in your hearts such as you have never known in this lifetime.

There will be light upon the Earth, and it will touch all those who have dwelled in darkness, and they will be called.

There will be a song that comes forth that all will immediately know and sing and share.

There will be gladness in the hearts of those whose lives have been lost.

There will be a call to come together, to celebrate.

How will this manifest? Many will ask, again and again, "How shall I know Him! How shall I know it is Him?"

We say unto you, if you are opened unto it and if your heart holds love and peace rather than fear and doubt and criticism and judgment, then, you shall know Him.

Will He do miracles? You are the miracle, and He will help you to know it. His presence will bring the light of God to those hearts and minds which are readied to receive same, and, when you see Him, you will know it is He and He will know you.

Will He do miracles? You are the miracle, and He will help you to know it.

April 11

Those of you who offer prayer for others, hear the song in your own heart, the song of your beauty, your uniqueness, and claim this first *before* you step forward to answer the call for prayer. For, wherein shall you find the Spirit of Father to be gifting in answer to the prayers requested of you, if not within thine own beauty and uniqueness?

Hear the song in your heart of your beauty and claim this before you step forward to answer the call for prayer.

April 12

When you look across the lands that comprise the sum of Earth, you can see the traditions, the belief structures, the habits, and the presence of those things which form the chains that limit. Do not believe for a moment that, because you are at a distance or that you are but one, that you have no power over helping those in distant lands who are entangled in the chains of habit or judgment or dogma or creed. For, it is what it is: the power of God that flows from within *you*, and you can touch them in a manner as you have been touched. And they can find the sacred silence and the peace and love and the grace of Father and, once it is known, it is ever known.

The tools with which you doet the work is no different than ours, here. The only difference that might exist is your willingness to claim them.

The tools with which you doeth the work is no different than ours. The only difference is your willingness to claim them.

April 13

Now is a time of significance for all of you. It is a time to bring forth the power of forgiveness from within the center of your being. Whether or not one accosts you or challenges you or, by the measure of the Earth, wrongs you, the greatest power that you have to answer such is forgiveness. Even were it to come to that point where you confront them and say, "I forgive you and I ask that you forgive me for that which I may have burdened you with. Know that my love for you cometh from Father and, as I choose to receive this, I also choose to share it and gift it to you. We are brethren, in the beginning and in the ending. Let us choose to see this all throughout the greater journey."

Now is a time to bring forth the power of forgiveness from within the center of your being.

April 14

Love yourselves, in order that you shall be able to know Father's love for you and that, together, this love can flow freely as a gentle breeze to wave across the lands to be taken into the Earth, itself, into the waters, the air, and all the creatures.

See your past as that upon which you now stand and that, alone. Dwell not long in the contemplation of it, lest it call you back to give it greater and greater energy. Be free.

Love yourselves, in order that you shall be able to know Father's love for you.

April 15

With a generous smile and love in the gaze with which He bathes them, He states, "The purpose of the journey is to know the truth of who and what you are in the eternal sense. "What you experience here," tapping the wood upon which He is perched, "and what you experience here," tapping His heart, "are actually no different. It is how you perceive them and what you decide to do with that perception that opens the way and makes it passable."

The purpose of the journey is to know the truth of who and what you are in the eternal sense.

April 16

If you can meet each challenge, if you can accept each opportunity presented by the forces within self, then, you can meet any faction, any experience, in any realm.

To be called by the Christ as His own, to be recognized, and for Him to prepare a place for thee in the Kingdom of God ... This means that thou art recognized as having accepted your oneness with God, and karma becomes an experience of past nature to you. It no longer is a needed tool. You will possess, then, grace. You will be able to use grace to serve, even further, others and yourself.

If you can meet each challenge, within, then, you can meet any faction, any experience, in any realm.

April 17

Your soul never leaves its position with God. Your soul is always in accord with God. What this is given to you for is to define the purpose of spiritual searching. The (as called by some) "Resurrection Day" intended is the purpose of seeking the Christ Light within. It is this Light and this, alone, that can bring to the mind and heart of an aware entity in physical body the full realization of the nature of their being.

The Resurrection, then, was purposely called in these terms as it was originally stated in great lengths, to just how to achieve complete union with the force of God and the love and kindness of the Master as manifested by God. In this, then, you will have a "Resurrection." It is planned. It is the purpose of your continued evolution.

But, in the sense that your physical body would be raised, the physical body is merely the collection of matter which has been formed by thought, and has drawn upon the forces of the plane that you exist in and given unto the materials of thought formation, and composited into a form which agrees with the rules or accepted thought of that plane. It would not be logical for you to wish to reassemble that physical body when the one that is truly your body has far more beauty and cannot be harmed or injured in the true sense when your mind is elevated to its likely position with God. Do you see?

It is the Christ Light and this, alone, that can bring to an aware entity the full realization of the nature of their being.

April 18

The Master did not say to those who asked him for healing, "Well, let's see, now … How long have you been wanting this healing? Are you prepared to continue to want it after you are healed? Will you watch your diet, your exercise schedule, and so forth?"

He asked only this: "Do you believe?"

When they answered, He stated clearly and concisely, then, "Go forth, for, thy faith has healed thee, and sin no more." He spoke not of injustices or violations of man's law in the literal impact of same but, rather, in the attitude that sin is a grief or guilt borne in the heart.

To be sure, there are righteous ways of living, and the teachers of righteousness have lain that path before thee and all to see. But it is, again, drawn back into the heart of the entity that, if they believe, then, it is that belief and their faith that can heal. Not a tool, not an implement, not a routine, not a dogma, a temple, a church, a crystal, an amulet, or whatnot, but the faith behind same. All the others are extensions or tools utilized by the belief within the soul and spirit of the entity involved.

He spoke not of violations of man's law but, rather, in the attitude that sin is a grief or guilt borne in the heart.

April 19

You are absorbing a certain degree of toxins from the atmosphere. There are, as we perceive them, several categories which are increasing in their levels of presence due to the shift in the wind patterns and such, which are a part of the Earth changes now taking place. If the body is kept in a state of activeness and the dietary is, of course, varied, you will provide the body with a broad array or spectrum of base elements, nutritives and such with which it can combat these new challenges from within.

It is not just that the body inhales these, though that's certainly a part of same, but these are also absorbed through the skin, the epidermal. They are carried in ground water and in drinking water. Often, they are absorbed by the plants, and so forth. Therefore, one cannot eliminate them, unless all of mankind would cooperate towards same. So, there must be the strengthening of the body, the mind, the spirit, to provide increased resilience and resistance to ward off these.

There must be the strengthening of the body, the mind, the spirit, to provide increased resilience and resistance.

April 20

As you would see areas that are out of harmony, that in and of itself is impossible.

So, if you see someone with dis-ease, they are experiencing an impossibility. Because they are Children of God, they have the power to create a lifetime wherein the impossible becomes possible and manifests. Here, beyond the finite, such a thing cannot be found. You cannot find something that is "imperfect" such as dis-ease implies.

So, when we say it is impossible, we are striving to tell you that this is a well person who is accepting the illusion of not being well. It would appear that mass-mind thought nourishes the claiming of a lack of perfection. See?

If you see someone with dis-ease, they are experiencing an impossibility.

April 21

Begin each day as though it is a new life. Open that life with your affirmation and connection to God. As you connect with God, then, you connect with all that you have been and all that you can be.

It is not difficult. It requires only that one look and ask, and in the asking, to be willing to receive.

Begin each day seeking.

Pause throughout the day to remember and strengthen that spirit within, no matter where you are or what you are about.

At the conclusion of the Earth day, prepare to return unto the Father, allowing your body to rest and freeing your spirit to journey into His embrace, knowing that He ever awaits thee.

Begin each day as though it is a new life.

April 22

Again, we encourage all of you consider that the potential for your meditations and prayer have not been greater in your lifetimes to date than these are in the moment. You are in those times of great expectation. You are potential contributors to the transformation of the Earth and the preparation of the Way. Be not faint-hearted. Neither single-eyed. Know that, as you can accomplish and claim in faith your oneness with all of existence, you shall help to awaken it unto itself. That, dear friends, is a goodly work in God's name. See?

You are potential contributors to the transformation of the Earth and the preparation of the Way.

April 23

Lucid dreaming is one's approach to the veil and then the passing through it, either knowingly passing through it or becoming aware that you have passed through it after you have so done.

The desired action here would be to become accomplished at this, that you could intentionally enter into a state of restfulness, a quieting of the body, of the conscious mind, of the emotions, from whence thee can go from this certain level to that certain level. Then, through the experiencing and developing of that pathway, to become as a tunnel of light, a pathway, a conduit, a line of light, a filament, a cord. Many titles are appropriate here. Many descriptions are acceptable. Then, as you do this, the veil becomes permeable.

Lucid dreaming is the command of one's spirit and one's mind to an equal level of vibration from whence one can perceive, or see.

Lucid dreaming is one's approach to the veil and then the passing through it.

April 24

Upon His entry there will be a period which follows of balancing, of choosing. And there will be the separation at the terminus of this period wherein those who are His will journey forth and make the way open and passable for those souls who have awakened from the beautiful dream to come unto the Earth, again, and bring love, and hope, and sweetness unto it that the Earth can be reborn and renewed, and that the seeds of hope might be sown all about.

First, there must come this time, this period (as you would call it) of balancing and choosing. See? Be mindful that those who are His, who bear His mark, will, then, be fully awakened and claim their heritage and, thus, they will be as He. See?

Upon His entry, there will be a call. Those who are seeking, those who are choosing, will be called unto Him. As this is accomplished, they will become claimants to the throne of God and they will walk beside Him as colleagues, as brother and sister ... as one.

Thereafter, there will be that intent to prepare the way and make it passable for those souls who are awakening, who have found forgiveness and hope and grace. These, then, when the time is aright, will enter and become those who bear the promise unto the Thousand Years of Peace.

Be mindful that those who are His, who bear His mark, will be fully awakened, claim their heritage and, will be as He.

April 25

Peter in his, indeed, innocent boldness, did be in askance of the Master, "Howbeit, O Lord, that it is stated, 'First must come Elias?'" To which the Master responded, "Indeed, truly, Elias must first come and restore all things."

So, there must come that which is a maker of peace, of harmony, that which prepares the way. Find in this that thee must put forth a certain effort in your own lives which makes the way perceptive, receptive, sensitive, and harmonious. This is a force of will which recognizes, in a state of profound truth, each certain thing for what it is truly, and each entity, great or lesser, man or woman, king or pauper, for what is in their heart much moreso than what is upon their body or among their possessions; and that this loving truth should reach unto them and invite or encourage that they make aright in their own temple (which is as to say their own home, their own dwelling, within their body, mind, and spirit of consciousness) so as to be receptive for those forces which will follow, borne by the Lamb of God, the Master; and that, so as this was affirmed as the Master came unto John for the anointment, the baptism, it was to affirm unto John that his work was well done, and completed nearly to its fullness.

So, we find, then, that for each of thee, the way must be made clear: The peacemaker must come before that which will gain. The prophet of truth and that which is of honor within each of thee must be willing to recognize every aspect that comprises your consciousness.

Thee must put forth effort in your own lives which makes the way perceptive, receptive, sensitive, and harmonious.

April 26

Know of yourselves that, as ye seek, you are known by those who seek to carry this spirit and this light to you.

Then, as ye would know yourselves, know that you can be present in, not only this event, but in any such event as there is import and desire in your heart to so do. For, believe not that those things which have gone before are concluded and gone forever, but know that ye can visit them and can be a part of that host, just so as those twelve who were seated with He who is the Light.

Know that you can be present in, not only this event, but in any event as there is import and desire in your heart to so do.

April 27

So, as ye next bring forth to the body its nourishment, think of that which has gone before making this nourishment possible. Think that, as ye take this physical substance into your physical body, there is a life-force or energy which is taken into your life-force or energy, so that, as ye consume this certain food or nourishment, ye cannot destroy it.

Know, then, that, so as ye give forth an action or a deed, it, too, cannot be destroyed, but is blessed by that which ye have taken in and intentionally and knowingly give forth.

Thus, so do all things live on through eternity, ever changing and moving, ever questing for a consciousness which shall bring them unto the return, as the logos finds itself ever returning unto itself and never ending.

As ye next bring to the body its nourishment, think of that which has gone before making this nourishment possible.

April 28

If ye would fall upon your pathway and are wearied and consider the alternative of not arising to carry on, know ever that, if ye seek and ask, one will come to thee as a comforter and will cleanse and anoint thee and will give thee healing so as ye need, such so as to give sufficient strength and more to arise and go forth. If, again and again, ye shall fall, then, call again and again, knowing that, no matter how often ye shall ask of the Father, He shall give it to thee.

What burden shall ye bear that cannot be overcome? A burden of stone or wood? These ye can find a means by which your strength can carry or move, for, the mind of man is inspired with creative thought, but what of those inner burdens, dear friends? These are those which the Master has shown to thee in this, perhaps, His greatest teaching. If ye have fear or doubt of self, then, this is as great, if not moreso, than that which the Master Himself bore on this day. Can ye call out and have one come to thy aid and lift this burden and carry same for thee? Of course, but ye must learn to hear and to see. Ye must open yourselves faithfully and with certainty, knowing that, as ye believe, then, that very belief enables you to accomplish any task whatsoe'er it might be.

No matter how often ye shall ask of the Father, He shall give it to thee.

April 29

The Master made a promise to the one who believed. To the one who did not believe, He spoke nothing. For, as ye are prepared and ask, it is given. But, if ye do not seek, if ye do not ask, whether ye believe or nay, how can it be given to thee? See?

In each experience, whether in the Earth or in other spheres, know that the heart of self bears within it that same force as is borne in the Master and as is evident in that as has been given:

This is not a heart which is saddened, which laments its lot. This is a heart which is filled with hope and joyful promise even as the body struggles. Know that even the best of those forces which can be found in all realms must expend, to some degree, an energy to grow. For, remember the Universal Laws ... One such requires that energy or action begets action, that, for each movement, there is a balancing movement. So, there must be the expenditure of a force in order to create a force or a movement.

If ye do not seek, if ye do not ask, whether ye believe or nay, how can it be given to thee? See?

April 30

Even as the Master bore the cross up the hill, His forbearance was one of peace, not of agony, not of fear, nor anything of such a nature. Those who were there and saw Him received a warm, knowing glance and a smile. Did His body bear the burden and weight of same? He honored the Law of the Earth, though He could have called out a simple word or two and it would have been lifted from Him and borne above Him as He might have chosen to walk straightaway up the hill.

It is good to remember that, whatsoever the experiences might be, the peace is the foundation and the joy comes from that wellspring. It is not so that one commandeth this or that, but, rather, that one sayeth a thing and it is. It comes from believing, but that believing is based upon the peace of God carried within, ever.

The Master walked the Earth in a state of complete peace, oneness, if you will. His only intention was and is to give. He is complete and was complete as He walked in flesh upon the Earth. The completeness, you see, builds the foundation for the possibility of anything.

Remember, whatsoever the experiences might be, the peace is the foundation and joy comes from that wellspring.

May 1

Oneness might be defined in these words, among many others to be sure...

Oneness is that state of being wherein you can be literally one with all of existence, finite and infinite, as you perceive it from Earth and, yet, so doing, not become that thing, or not become individualized in the sense of separation.

Oneness is the state of being that recognizes your uniqueness and the uniqueness of all, and places this within the treasure house within eternally.

Oneness is the state of consciousness and acceptance that knows all is of God, all is God.

Oneness is the ability to recognize in a brother or sister that which is you.

Oneness is that state of being that recognizes that definition does not mean limitation.

Oneness is the state of being and consciousness that ever seeks to know itself and, so doing, realizes that, to know oneness is to know all aspects of it.

From this, then, is born the realization for each entity, each soul, that, until self is known and loved, until self can be seen in its past actions, its current thoughts, and its considerations for that which lies ahead, and take all of these in the spirit of Grace ... only then is oneness truly possible for that individual, that entity, that soul.

Oneness is the ability to recognize in a brother or sister that which is you.

May 2

It is said by many that these are times of wondrous
change and wondrous awakening.

Change, awakening ... These do not point to the retention
of the old. They do not point to becoming entrenched in the
familiar or that which was. Be free and be, as the Master gave
it, unburdened, that you can seek and knock and ask that it
can be given to you.

Change, awakening ... These do not point to the retention of
the old.

May 3

There is no call greater than that call given to self. There is the illusion of the greater call coming from without.

There is no circumstance outside of self which should be given demand or authority over self and the pursuit of that which is righteous for self.

So then, as another, or others, come unto thee, noting the light and life pouring from the wellspring within thee, and say unto thee, "Sister/brother, give unto me of thy wellspring," and thou doeth this in His name, thereafter, as they turn about so nourished and so gifted, must *they* determine the outcome of the gifts they are given.

There is no call greater than that call given to self.

May 4

All Forces are ever seeking to evolve into a state of order and harmony. Those Forces which do not seek to evolve, perpetuate discord.

If you are seeking evolvement, then, seek a state of harmony.

If you are seeking evolvement, then, seek a state of harmony.

May 5

The nature of reality is dependent upon what one has experienced within reality, don't you think so?

The reality that you have experienced, then, is what you see through, as a sort of window pane of colored glass or some such ... (haven't the right words here).

So, if one has their reality, based on what they have experienced, and they see through that, hear through it, and all the other stuff that goes with that, then, it follows, quite certainly, that, unless one has very similar experiences in reality as that one, there may be disagreement. See?

The nature of reality is dependent upon what one has experienced within reality.

May 6

If you could actually see Him and He was there and touched you, and you asked Him a certain thing, what would that thing be? Would it be, "O Lord, I am in need of this," or would it be, "Lord, help me to set myself free and be one with you."

The relevance of the material becomes transient. As one seeks the greater, then, the material is seen in a beautiful light. From that position of oneness with God and that of faith and peace, the material, the physical, can flow easily; but fear, you see, will veil this.

Free yourself and become at peace and, when you are at peace, the greater will be given. It is difficult to fill a cup that shakes with fear.

It is difficult to fill a cup that shakes with fear.

May 7

In the journey called life it is often difficult to discern the reality of what is.

Allow yourselves to be at peace, for whatsoever you conceive, whatsoever you accept, can and does become your reality. The building of consciousness within brings this to clarification and empowers you to realize that, from your eternal nature as a child of God, this will become an important steppingstone to those works and those joyful experiences that lie beyond.

Thus, be of good cheer. See? All is well.

Allow yourselves to be at peace, for whatsoever you conceive, whatsoever you accept, can and does become your reality.

May 8

The Christ lives on as the spark of life born in each living being in Earth.

So is it, then, as well, with those who have departed the Earth, and who are in varying degrees of limitation, also called darkness. Yet, within the very depths of same is the Light of God. And within the very highest points of the Light is the Darkness of God, for, they are not alien, not meant ... nor *are* they ... in opposition.

Within the very depths of limitation is the Light of God.

May 9

All prayers should, first, be directed to God.

All prayers should, first, be directed to God.

There is a period of time wherein the soul, upon departure from the Earth, will linger ... generally, within the realms of the Earth plane. If the period of bereavement and grief and abashed love is too long, too intense, the soul will be, in essence, held somewhat in realms close to the Earth plane, unable to continue.

Search through your minds for the happiest experiences that you can recall between you and the departed entity. Think of the events, the moments, the words which were exchanged, which promoted happiness and harmony. Once this feeling is created, then, release the actual words or events, and hold the feelings. Then, think of the entity's name, and then state a prayer similar to this:

Eternal God, we give to Thee now this most beloved soul, (state their name). We pray Thee now to guide, to counsel, as you often have while this soul was in the Earth plane. We ask humbly that you take them in loving kindness and warmth – as they shall always be held in our heart – and deliver them unto those purposes, and those kindred souls with whom they shall now serve in accord with Thy will. For this we thank Thee ever, Father. Amen.

With such a prayer, you release them to their benefit, and to God. Incidentally, you also assure – practically without exception – an open line of communication of sorts, between yourself and that soul.

If the period of bereavement is too long, too intense, the soul will be held in realms close to the Earth, unable to continue.

May 11

It is recognized that, upon the Earth plane, there will be those achievements and those pathways wherein mankind will dwell upon the Earth in great harmony. The Earth has, early in its creation, been determined (or you would prefer perhaps, been *assigned*) as a planet of dwelling for great harmony and great beautification of the souls involved. During these times, then, there will be many great souls, as you would define this, who shall enter the Earth plane, contribute, and manifest to this purpose.

There will be many great souls who shall enter the Earth plane, contribute, and manifest to this purpose.

May 12

Every obstacle has within its structure a portal of opportunity. If you allow yourself to be captivated by dreams of the past, hopes and visions of what might have been, you are not opening the doorway, you are not entering the portal of what can be.

If you allow yourself to be captivated by dreams of the past, you are not entering the portal of what can be.

May 13

Those things which are dependent upon the choices, the will, and the aspects of others outside of self cannot be taken within and made perfect and whole and joyful, for, they are under the dominion of the free will of those who are also children of God.

To have the peace, it must be based upon that which is the foundation in you, not based on something without.

To have the peace, it must be based upon that which is the foundation in you, not based on something without.

May 14

In order that one can accomplish the state of joy and the attitude that knows self to be at one with God, there must first be the realization that you are what you believe.

You are what you believe.

May 15

The amount of time for manifestation of what is being sought is directly relevant to the certainty of that which is being sought and the belief that supports it. See?

The amount of time for manifestation of what is sought is directly relevant to the certainty of the belief that supports it.

May 16

What you do, do it with peace and joy within. Even if it is not your primary choice, see it as an opportunity.

If you can do what is before you and maintain an attitude of peace and joy, then, do it. ... peace, primarily, for, joy comes from peace, see.

The attitude must hold abundance of peace and joy. Then, whatsoever works you do would be in that same manner, and the gladness of your spirit within will shine and will be as a light to attract that which you need and the greater. See?

The gladness of your spirit within will shine and will be as a light to attract that which you need and the greater.

May 17

Reincarnation is not mandatory. It is not forced upon any soul. It is, rather, a choice made by that soul at a point or viewing of the soul's past experiences. A soul may choose to wait for some period of time before reentering the Earth plane, or may choose to function or exist in a form of existence on another plane, such as planes very similar to what you would call material or mental existence.

An example here might be: An individual, having had a past incarnative experience on the Earth plane, arriving, then, at a point of existence that would be after the experience you would call death would assess their position best upon these new experiences. They might choose, at that point to exist within the sphere of mental existence of the Earth plane moreso than its physical sphere for contributing to others in one manner or another and, thus, balance through this shared experience, some spiritual growth or some increased awareness of their own need.

Reincarnation is not mandatory. It is not forced upon any soul. It is, rather, a choice made by that soul.

May 18

In order to be fulfilled, you must be fulfilled. See? Fulfillment expected from without is temporal. True fulfillment that is based on you, within, and your oneness with God within from a state of peace, and that peace knowing ever that all is well.

Fulfillment expected from without is temporal.

May 19

All of you who hear and feel what we are giving: We call to you to remember ... Remember the beauty of your uniqueness.

Remember the beauty of your uniqueness.

May 20

Periodically throughout the Earth day, good to reaffirm
your oneness with God.
A moment's pause, close the eyes ...
Thank you, Father-Mother-God, for being with me.
Claiming is an empowering action. So few recognize this,
yet, its power is inestimable. See?

Periodically throughout the Earth day, good to reaffirm your
oneness with God.

May 21

You asked about the role of praise and thanks unto God for healing ... If one weakens that thought even just that whit or just this small fragment by relating the healing to the entity who is the channel and not unto God, then, the source of that light, the power of that which is the perfect energy, is diminished. This makes for the weakening of that work.

The prayer, the praise, is the affirmation of one unto the Source of all. See? It is not difficult or complex. It is merely to affirm that God is that source which is the provider of all that is given and all that is received.

We wish to make that point very clear so as not to be misleading ... Each entity who functions as a channel of blessings is, in effect, the image of God at that moment. If this is not sustained, then, when that which is the physical apparition and reality in the three-dimensional sense returns, there is the difficulty and the question and the subsequent doubt, and doubt is that which weakens any energy, and any force.

It is the purpose of praise and prayer and thanks unto God to eliminate or to at least minimize that potential doubt.

The prayer, the praise, is the affirmation of one unto the Source of all.

May 22

The impossible is always possible when one believes that the possible is possible.

But when one believes the possible is impossible, what possibility is there of anything being possible?

The impossible is always possible when one believes that the possible is possible.

May 23

All children of God were created in a single moment of time. Each is the equal of the other, not only in your terms of age, but in equal standing unto God, for, in this instant you all came into being.

So, you might ponder, if this is so, how might each appear to have reached different positions in respect to the universe? This is more accurately described as the degree of awareness of each of you, for, throughout time as you would define it to this point which you call the now, you have undergone an involved series of events to generate awareness. What is this awareness? It is a series of many experiences, for, how can an entity have understanding, if there is not experience to build this upon? So, God's infinite patience permits you eternity to achieve these experiences. You have ofttimes referred to this as incarnations ... the process and repetitive process of experiences end to end.

Your existence at the present is only but one drop of water in an ocean.

All children of God were created in a single moment of time. Each is the equal of the other, and equal unto God.

May 24

No effort is without purpose. Even the most saddening
event in this existence has purpose.

When you have done a large wrong by your society's
standards, this is not a wrong in God's eyes, do you see, for
this is progress and, as these individuals might judge you,
God does not judge you. He allows you to assess between
these existences at times of greater awareness how you have
progressed during this time of testing.

No effort is without purpose. Even the most saddening event
in this existence has purpose.

May 25

What of karma and karmic debt? It is true, that such terms do exist, and it is further true that they are a reality but, mark these words well ... they need not be so. For, if you now look upon these past wrongdoings (as you have adjudged them) and say, "Oh, my. How might I have wronged my neighbor or my wife in such a way?" recognizing that you would not have wished to have this happen ... to you, that is atonement within your own mind.

But, you must accept this. Words alone cannot conquer this attitude of mind. If you cannot firmly accept this, you will carry this forward to another time. Between existences you will review these things carefully, but it is of far greater difficulty to reconcile them at that time for the reason that you must continually test them in what is considered your conscious realm. When it is so tested, if you pass this test (by your own standards), you will then free yourself from this bondage.

When you hold your hand outstretched to a stranger and, for no visible purpose or reason, give assistance to one in need, this frees each of you from some of this bondage. You see, this is another principle revealed: It is greater to give than it is to receive, but there are times when receiving in a certain way are also of great benefit. It is difficult in your physical world to comprehend a return for giving, but, most assuredly, you reap a grand harvest.

If you look upon "wrongdoings," recognizing you would not have wished to have this happen is atonement.

May 26

We know, dear friends, and we speak this to all of you, of the nature of dwelling in the Earth. We know that the illusion is all-powerful. We know that the limitations and the conditions of existence in Earth impose their demands or requirements upon your minds and your hearts. We do not fault the attitude, nor the law of man, but neither shall we weaken in our teaching and our presentation to you of the beauty and the eternal joy of the Laws of God. We can only state to you again that, so as ye would, each one, apply these, so shall ye become workers in His light.

So as ye would each one apply the Laws of God, so shall ye become workers in His light.

May 27

Remember many of the Master's teachings about love:
Love can set you free. Love is the power that heals. Love
is the power that surmounts all and challenges nothing. Love
exists as a small particle or a great mountain within all.
The Master demonstrated love and the power of it, repeatedly. Now, perhaps, you can begin the process of following His guidance.
Pray on this. Meditate on it. Set yourselves free. See?

The Master demonstrated love and the power of it, repeatedly. Pray on this. Meditate on it. Set yourselves free. See?

May 28

These are good times to continually remember that meditation is not just a time of rest. It is not just an experience wherein you call out to God and hope to hear a response. Meditation is also exercise to the soul, to the spirit of Self.

Meditation is exercise to the soul, to the spirit of Self.

148

May 29

Think of yourself as rising up in a very beautiful warm-air balloon. The limitations are the ballast. As you jettison the ballast, the balloon rises higher. Do not criticize yourself. Do not continue to carry the ballast that prevents your beautiful balloon from rising into embrace by Father. Set yourself free by choosing Freedom.

Set yourself free by choosing Freedom.

May 30

As the quickening of spirit and spiritual forces moves in utter harmony with this time of change, know that it is an opportunity for a new beginning.

And that its newness is derived from the fact that you are now able to see and know many things which were fragmentary in the past.

And that the beginning signifies the opportunity to correlate these into a new way of life.

And that nothing can become manifest in the Earth or in any realm until it is held as a thought-form of sorts in the minds and hearts of the beholders.

And that this, then, could be looked upon as the seed which will bear forth a new way, a new life, and all that is associated with those terms.

Nothing can become manifest in the Earth until it is held as a thought-form the minds and hearts of the beholders.

May 31

The only true quest is that which is within. The completion or fulfillment of that quest should shine from the within to the without, not the opposite ... that the shining is dependent upon something without.

The only true quest is that which is within.

June 1

If you are seeking to develop Self, then, see faith as one of those keys.

The scholar has chosen a path of learning because they know they will have greater potential, greater comprehension, greater wisdom and, as the result, they will be more joyful, more secure, more productive, more wealthy (any of these ... it matters not, see); but they know inwardly that, by choosing such a path, they will gain in some way.

So, the more you can apply faith in your daily life, then, know the moreso will you gain. If you see faith as it is – a gift of Spirit, a tool given to you from God that, when you claim it, it is all-powerful – then, you will wish to use it more and more. As you do, it opens many opportunities to you. That faith, as applied, becomes productive of fruits, of results, and you get greater and greater as the result.

The technician, the worker, becomes more skilled with the application of their talents. Why would God give you less with something as precious as your Eternal Spirit?

Faith is the pathway, which, when followed, will lead you to God. See?

Faith is the pathway, which, when followed, will lead you to God.

June 2

The material and the literal accomplishments in the materiality of the Earth do not endure beyond that lifetime, save for the effects of same upon the soul or souls involved with such, but the acts of kindness, the expressions of support and encouragement do.

It is upon the arm of those that thou have helped that ye might enter easily into the kingdom of our Father, not on Earthly accomplishment. Measure not your life comparatively in that sense but, rather, in the sense of feeling right about self, feeling good about the things that thou doeth and the support and loving kindness given to others ... even if they don't merit it, see.

It is upon the arm of those that thou have helped that ye might enter easily into the kingdom of our Father.

June 3

Ever let there be in your heart and mind a sacred place in which you can find compassion, and understanding, wisdom, and the truth of the infinite nature of your being as a child of God. Let these be the tools with which you fashion the life which you are now upon as a journey.

Ever let there be in your heart and mind a sacred place.

June 4

Everything in existence is for you. Whether it is adjudged good or bad, it is there for you. In the process of searching out and finding your place of Oneness with the Creative Force, with God, you will undoubtedly pass through much of creation that does not outwardly seem to impart that which is of the Light, or even joyful. But it is there for you. Gratitude is empowering. It is the recognition by a child of God of their power, and of the omnipotent presence of the Light and power of God in the entirety of their life.

Everything in existence is for you. Whether it is adjudged good or bad, it is there for you.

June 5

Ministry is to self first ... claiming the joy, not claiming the limitations of others.

Ministry is to self first ... claiming the joy, not claiming the limitations of others.

June 6

It is well for you, each one, to remember who and what you are. Even though the conditions which surround you in Earth may prevail such so as to dissuade you from your highest intent, know in your hearts and minds that you shall succeed and you shall gain that enlightenment and those gifts which the Father has promised unto thee, every one.

Even though, here and there, there may appear to be from time to time a limiting act, a thought less than the highest, or a deed performed out of habit or haste, let not these shadows darken the hope nor the spirit which is in you. Rather, then, choose to know that thou art already within the Father's kingdom and that thy sojourn in the Earth is intended to be a helpmeet to that understanding.

Therefore, were you not to meet those challenges, those opportunities, or those events or entities which would test thee, then, there could not be ultimately the tempering of that steel which is so pure within.

Know in your hearts that you shall succeed and gain that enlightenment and those gifts the Father has promised thee.

June 7

This is that time for you to reach within and find your potential, and we do not mean this in the confined sense of a small, neatly packaged ability, talent, or such, that you and you alone possess. It is greater than this. It is the potential of the unlimited Self, likened unto the seeds which God Himself has sown into you at the moment of your creation, or more accurately, your awakening.

For, consider, if it be true that God always has been, always is, then, if we are born of God we, too, have dwelled within Him. But the awakening of the particle can contribute to the sum of the whole of same and, the greater is the growth of that particle, logically, obviously, the more resplendent becomes the whole. Therein, lies one of the magnificent keys of opportunity for all of you at this very moment and henceforth.

This is that time for you to reach within and find your potential, the potential of the unlimited Self.

June 8

The teachers of righteousness are in the Earth. They are being called to awaken again. The wisdoms of old are coming to the fore. In them and about them, are the opportunities which, in their manifestation, can make the Way passable. If it is to be so, think you not that it must, first, be passable within them? That were it not so, they, in their works and in their lives, would be divided? Do you understand this?

Journeys into and out of the soul will become more and more common in the Earth from this very moment forward. Many unique works, many remarkable accomplishments, are manifesting and shall manifest with a rapidity that should spawn joy to those of you who have the sight to see them. You can take these works, the collective works of truth and right-eousness, and bring them back into the Earth. Many of you are awakening to this, even as we speak and, while you might seem separate in your focus and in your individual works, you will see, more and moreso as time continues in the immediate future, that this is one work.

Journeys into and out of the soul will become more and more common in the Earth from this very moment forward.

June 9

We see Father in you. We see Father in each other. To be with Father is to be with all, for there is naught but Father.

All that you are and all that you experience is within Father. All that lies without, as far as your instruments can perceive and your minds can calculate, is within Father and, beyond this, is Father, and that which is beyond the known or calculated is the glory of God awaiting you ... His children.

The gifts of our Father cannot be given names. They cannot be given descriptive terminology. The glory of His gifts to you can only be known by being one with them. The pathway to this is the Path of Peace within you.

To be with Father is to be with all, for, there is naught but Father.

June 10

You may find at times that it seems quite difficult to build a dream. You may find at times that where you are and who you are and what is involved with you in your life lacks a certain luster, vibrancy, or beauty that was the epitome of your dreams in years before. If this is so for you, consider for a moment, is this the dream that you have always sought and, now, in the realization of it, the sweetness, the luster, is not as you had anticipated?

It is of great importance to all ... Always renew and rejoice in your dreams each and every Earth day, for, so doing gives life to them. Even though it may appear that you have gained all that you have sought, or reached the accomplishment of those things you set out to do, ever are the greater just beyond where you are.

In the teachings that are held sacred all throughout the Earth, you will find that the journey is an eternal one. Thus, see this and know it to indicate to you not to become lost in an accomplishment, but inspired by it. Realize that, as there has been an accomplishment, whether great or small, this evidences to you that building the dream, the intent, the hopeful anticipation, is the first step to bringing it into reality. Never stop too long, before you renew the dream that is greatest of all: that you've reached that which is the full potential of your being.

_____

Renew the dream that is greatest of all: that you've reached that which is the full potential of your being.

June 11

Faith is a power that is borne on the wings of peace . . .
Are you at peace?

You do not have to speak to a thing to call it into action
on your behalf. You have only to be at peace within yourself
and know your oneness with All.

The All ... It is this that moves the mountains from there
to here. It is this that calls out to the elements and calms
them. It is this that speaks to the *dis*-ease within an entity and
frees it, that it can be transformed into ease.

Faith is a power that is borne on the wings of peace.

June 12

In order that one can insure that they have overcome a limiting past emotion, there must be brought before self those experiences which are likened unto the earlier ones that shall test, that shall provide the means from which you can discern the success or additional need for further effort on your part with regard to emotional limitation. Whether those emotions be fear, anger, or whatnot, such are, in their basic structure, depleting to the potential of self, that the power of the soul-consciousness within self, even though expressed in a finite body, needs to have its channel or vehicle through which that power can come forth as an end result or work.

Another way of stating this is that, in order for you to accomplish your soul's purpose in the Earth, these events as have transpired in your life to the present have been important steppingstones. But they are steppingstones only if one views them as such. Looked at from an improper perspective, they would be seen as obstacles, a wall or some such. The best way to deal with emotion on a day-to-day basis is to accept it. Denial of emotion simply buries same and causes it to spring forth in an unexpected outcropping. When one recognises events, activities, tendencies, habits, or whatnot, this lessens the power or hold which they have upon self. As you affirm the presence of a certain emotion, then you are placing it outside of self, as an object or thing. Denying its presence is burying it within. We pray the difference is clear here

----

Events in your life to the present have been important steppingstones, but only if one views them as such.

June 13

The majesty of the children of God is so beautiful for us to behold. In the Earth, so many cover this majesty with the illusion of finiteness.

So many cover their majesty with the illusion of finiteness.

June 14

Allow yourself to give up doubt and fears ... fears, as some of you hold, of being "seen as wrong." The judgment of self is the greatest limitation for many, many entities. Your energy is the collection of experiences that you have had during this journey in Earth. Do you see this? Look upon these experiences and strive to set them free. In other words, look to the creation of the experiences, whether they were and are good or bad, joyful or not so. Reach out to them and bless them and set them free ... calling the energy to the forefront and forgiving yourself and forgiving it, and calling for the Father to set it free to be that pure energy.

The judgment of self is the greatest limitation for many, many entities.

June 15

Generally, massage is good for all disease in the essence
that disease is the lack of ease in the physical body. That
which has precipitated the dis-ease, of course, may not be
directly affected by the massage, but the conditions at the
physical level and also at the emotive and mental level are
generally affected in a positive sense by the action of
massage.

There is the basic need of love and compassion between
entities on all realms. We cannot emphasize this with
sufficient strength ... all realms. So it is, then, that the benefit
of massage is so broad we would have to state that, generally,
it applies for all dis-eases, even a toothache, as one might
think it an odd prescription for such an ailment.

The benefit of massage is so broad we would have to state
that, generally, it applies for all dis-eases, even a toothache.

June 16

Prayer is the promise of God that He will always be with you.

If you ask, you have it. If you believe that you have it, it becomes reality. If you doubt, it becomes an energy which may manifest here or there, today or tomorrow, or when the conditions are such for it to be accepted without a violation of the right of free will or karma or spiritual intent.

Prayer is the promise of God that He will always be with you.

June 17

The body is affected by varying elemental forces, none the least of which is the karma: the thought-pattern which is carried over by that entity, that soul, into this incarnation. Then, this has an effect upon the base cell structure, determining a slightly higher acidity or a slightly higher alkalinity. The continuation of these forces is perpetuated by, in effect, the spiritual pattern that is to influence that sojourn, that lifetime and, further, those thought-forms as are prevalent in the Earth plane during that sojourn. Also, the thoughts, attitudes, and emotions of those entities who are closest will, obviously, have a more direct effect than those which are a bit more distant. ...

The soul moving through the Earth plane will accumulate certain habits and patterns, likes and dislikes, and these all are associated with the preemptive (you might state) pattern of the karma, the thought with which that soul enters.

So, then, in order to change a basic pattern or the skein from which the life pattern is woven, one must return to form a change, a new habit, a new vision, at the spiritual level. Just so very often given is that to meditate and to oft times be in quiet reflection and/or prayer is to begin the state of ease or healing.

To change the skein from which the life pattern is woven, one must return to form a change at the spiritual level.

June 18

As we would seek to assist lovingly and humbly, we would point to the acid-alkaline balance in the body as one of the most powerful tools that each of ye have in which ye can manipulate or change the state of ease in the body.

The acid-alkaline balance in the body is one of the most powerful tools ye have to change the state of ease in the body.

June 19

Prayer differs from simple thought in the aspect that prayer is the invocation of your spiritual body to be in harmony with the mental, or the reverse. It is the movement of force from your spiritual consciousness, which prevails, then, upon the mental to project a thought-form in its purest form.

The moreso one carefully verbalizes and feels the prayer, the purer and more profound and, consequently, the more powerful, is the powerful thought-form.

That's essentially what you are doing in the mechanics of it. It's building the spiritual pattern and, by the mind's will, allowing that pattern to be accepted in the mental body. And allowing the spiritual force to extend or to unite with the mental as a singular thrust or a singular receptor to function, then, in accordance with that of the plan or schedule which is the intent.

Prayer differs from thought in that prayer is the invocation of your spiritual body to be in harmony with the mental.

June 20

The emphasis upon the Earth being the home to all should be underscored here, and should be a part of the global prayer. This, we should think, is all too obvious. See?

The emphasis upon the Earth being the home to all should be underscored and should be a part of the global prayer.

June 21

Change is opportunity.

There are those who look upon change with fear, with sadness, because, in the face of change and the release of the old, the familiar is seen to be dissipating and, in its stead, comes the unknown. We here, and those of you who know these truths, can proclaim the opportunity that is in the change over and over again and, yet, the fixation upon keeping the status quo, as you call it, is so powerful within some individuals, some groups, some classes and masses, that they will hear not, for, they have not the spiritual ear with which to hear. Their senses are dedicated to their current and previous position ... some, out of a desire for dominance, for control, for power, for affluence beyond the measure of any individual's need. Others will have this sort of limitation because they know not the glory of their own spirit, the joy of fellowship with those who now seem foreign to their life, to their way of thinking, and to that which is endearing to them.

Thus, we, humbly and gently, encourage you to open your hearts and minds to that which is new. As you look upon the past and see it to be good, then, place it where it belongs—as the foundation upon which the light and hope of the future can rest.

We encourage you to open your hearts and minds to that which is new, and place the past where it belongs.

June 22

Joy is a state of being.
When you claim joy, is it strong enough to be complete within you and unto you? Or is it dependent upon others?

Is your joy strong enough to be complete within you, or is it dependent upon others?

June 23

It is the comfort of familiarity to remain in some form of dis-ease. Not to suggest that you believe that you've earned it, but that the expression of creativeness does just that—it's an absolute thing.

When you recognize that you are the creator and that you can begin to change that which is under your purview, then, this begins the creative process that can reach far beyond the singular expression or purview of one entity, and begin to impact and bless others.

You are the creator and you can begin to change that which is under your purview, and begin to impact and bless others.

June 24

Those of you who are feeling and reflecting on the subtle-
ties of memory, of knowing, of being awakened, we offer to
you this: You are being called. You are being lifted up.

Then, from this, hear the resonance from within and look
about your life and see, "Now I am awakening to become the
master of my domain. I do not violate, neither do I transgress.
But I do not yield my right nor my light to that which would
seek to limit me."

Sing the song of your freedom. Celebrate and rejoice. Be
glad of heart and know that the greater cometh.

I am the master of my domain. I do not I transgress. Neither
do I yield my light to that which would seek to limit me.

June 25

We cannot give to you any greater than we have in the past in terms of demarcation of time, nor can we state with any authority that this or that shall come to pass on this certain day. It is you, dear friends, who have that potential to bring about peace, within and without, that the energies of the Earth will feel the blessing of your presence rather than the conflict that is so oft present between you.

Celebrate life and see the Earth as a precious gift, for, that is what it is. Its Beauty is dependent upon you for its continuity of existence. When this is seen and claimed, then, the beauty of the concert of God's intent is manifest, and all will benefit from it.

It is you, dear friends, who have that potential to bring about peace, within and without, the Earth will feel your blessing.

June 26

No power is greater than the power you are willing to claim.

No light can ever be any brighter than that light you find in the sanctuary within your own being and which you bring forth.

No wisdom is clearer, sharper, keener than that which you have gained through the journeys of your spirit, the experiences of your current lifetime brought to the altar of truth and honor within, and carefully weighed and measured, that your path becomes guided by this wisdom, and your service, thereafter great.

No song can be sung sweeter than the song of your own heart when it is filled with the joy and resonance of love. For, love is the song of God spoken in the Word of God which goes forth from you in your being, in your word, your action and deed. Love is the light of God, and it penetrates and transcends all illusion that such be revealed for its own nature and intent.

No song can be sung sweeter than the song of your own heart when it is filled with the joy and resonance of love.

June 27

Illusions do not, in the sense of their individuality, bear you harm. To the contrary, they bear you opportunity.

For, if you can interact on the stage of illusion, the drama of interacting in the finite, and emerge from same with the light of your spirit just a whit or two in greater luminosity, then, in the next drama, that greater light will be yours, your right to bear. Each successive drama, increased in its luminosity individually and collectively shall bring all souls that much closer to the point of ultimate return and oneness with God.

Illusions, the drama of interacting in the finite, do not bear you harm. To the contrary, they bear you opportunity.

June 28

The Earth is in transition. It is in transition in part because it has not been kept in balance, but not that, alone. The Earth is in transition because it is meant to grow, to change, to become renewed, elevated, expanded.

The Earth is in said point of transition to portend those times of glorious discovery. These will not be limited to those of the faithful, as they are called, but to all those who are willing to seek and know, and who are willing to hold the peace of God within themselves and to reach within for the mainstay of their truth and faith and love. Then, these will see and know these new times which lie ahead. They will be opened to all who are willing to receive them by the Master, the Christ, and those who are with Him.

The Earth is in transition to portend those times of glorious discovery.

June 29

The limitations (as some would perceive them) that entities experience are actually gifts, but the gifts are not manifested because they are still in the form of a limitation. Once that one who has such sees it, knows it, and claims it, then, they can withdraw their life energy from it, and it becomes as a foundational stone upon which they can ascend to higher realms of consciousness. See

---

The limitations that people experience are gifts ... gifts not manifested because they are still in the form of a limitation.

June 30

If an entity is injured, you soothe them with healing waters. Then, when in meditation or prayer for another, see waters of light cascading down over the entity who is in need swirling about them, penetrating every fiber of their being. Speak to the waters of each cell. Call them out if they are errant and purify the waters, displacing the dross and the illusion. If there is one whose body is withered, restore it by replenishing the waters of their fiber, of their mind, and heart, and of their spirit.

If a traveler, wearied by his journey, should behold thee and ask thee for a cup of water, thou would surely give this unto him, would thee not? How be it, then, that thou perceiveth an entity who is in a state of dis-ease different than a weary traveler? They ask of thee for the cup of water. Can thee do less than give this unto them?

The moreso a rivulet within thee is used, the greater and deeper shall its channel become. The moreso the waters of spirit pour through thee, the closer ye shall find self moving unto its Source. If thee and the waters of eternal life become as one in works of joy and light to the Father's name, they wilt ever support thee and know thee to be their own.

The moreso the waters of spirit pour through thee, the closer ye shall find self moving unto its Source.

July 1

How do you keep your joy today, in the knowledge that the greater joy lies beyond, and here in the Earth there is challenge, limitation, frustration, sadness, avarice, lust, disease, and so on and so forth?

These qualifiers of God's potential do not exist in the realms of Light. Why? What is their purpose? Then, ask self, "What is their purpose here in the Earth? What do they serve in my own mind and heart? Do I depend upon this thing or that thing, or this or that person, or this or that object or accomplishment for my joy?"

If so, it is best that you do not cling to that as the source of your joy, for, you will limit yourself.

Expect joy to be in all things, and it will be and, when you are challenged by that which appears to be far less than that expectation, do not own it. Do not claim it. See it as that which is before you and before others as the rain of experience. Through that flow of experience you must always realize, if you are to be what your potential is, that these are the things for which you entered and these are the things which you have asked for.

If you approach them with the proper mindset and the proper spirit, they will melt away before you. That is one of the "tests" of a master soul or a step-away master soul. See?

If you approach challenges with the proper mindset and the proper spirit, they will melt away before you.

July 2

Think love ... self-containing, veritable unlimited source or flow of love. The capacity within you is beyond comprehension. So don't worry that you'll use it up. See? Put a little bit of love before you in everything that you do, and the effects of what you do will bear that energy and must, under the Law, not only bear a blessing to those who receive same but, in return, to you as well.

Put a little bit of love before you in everything that you do.

July 3

Fear creates an imbalance, or is an accelerant to a state of imbalance. Then, recognize one of the greater remedies for most all things that are amiss is joy and peace.

Joy comes from the state of realizing that you are a child of God, and claiming that and living it and being it ... living a state of peace and living the attitude of happiness, an attitude of expectancy, joyfully ... believing in self, not looking to be as another is, or many others are, but looking at self as that creation of God which is a treasure to God.

Were it so that God wished to have all perfect in a certain categorical definition, then, it would be so. It is not so. The perfection lies within each individual. When this is seen and claimed, then, the beauty of the concert of God's intent is manifest, and all will benefit from it.

Believe in self. Look at self as that creation of God which is a treasure to God.

July 4

In an ordered structure, things need to conform in order to be in harmony with law. Law is thought of to be a restricting, guiding, often valuable, course of thought, but God's Law is that each soul is completely independent, is completely without restriction, limitation, or reservation. He is as one with His own being. So, His Law is to preserve the total freedom of your consciousness.

God's Law is to preserve the total freedom of your consciousness.

July 5

When you reach the point that you know faith so well that anything you do, any thought that you think, is viewed, not only from that perspective of your mind's storehouse of knowledge, but also from your spirit's perspective of what you truly are, then your life becomes the living example as you see in your Brother, the Master, the Christ. You know, then, that God is the source and that you are His child and His instrument, as you so will it, through which and by which all things are possible. That is faith in its summated form. It is the claiming of your heritage.

As you exercise it more and more in greater and greater depth and breadth throughout your life, ultimately it shall become a continual part of all that you do and think. Then, shall you become one in spirit with God. See?

God is the source and you are His instrument, as you so will it, through which and by which all things are possible.

July 6

Those of you who walk the path with faithfulness and endure the challenges and the misunderstandings and the conflicts and all that sort that the powers of domination seek to impose upon you, we are ever with you. We say to you: Righteousness shall prevail.

Those of you who walk the path with faithfulness and endure the challenges, we are ever with you.

July 7

Create for self a willingness, a desire, to reach beyond self in terms of what you see, what you feel, and how you relate to the forces of Earth. This maketh the path open for the Law, which is as the Word and the mantle or staff, and anointment, which is the recognition of thy presence and thy oneness or bond with God's will.

Thee must elevate above that which is common or preponderant in life.

Create for self a desire to reach beyond self in terms of what you see and feel, and how you relate to the forces of Earth.

July 8

The Master called several together, a goodly number, actually, and there was the exploration of that which was known that which Our Lord knew would unfold. Within the beauty of Universal Law, many souls began to focus their light and their oneness with God in a manner of speaking that perhaps could not be understood in your current time, but may well be understood by some of you very soon:

They went forward into those times. And, where it was known that the Law would be manipulated or misused, they sowed seeds of the Promise.

In effect, we could summate this by stating, into each challenge that was known to be held in the hearts of the forces of opposition did they place into the potential for the future a gift, that there could be, ever, as each one of their own beloved grouping might, through their dedication and willingness to follow these paths of limitation and finiteness … as they were challenged, they would also know that a gift also was mandated to be present under the Law, as these had sown same.

Into each challenge that was known did they place the future a gift, that, as they were challenged, a gift also was sown.

July 9

Know that you are creating ... in your thoughts, in your words, in your deeds. They are according to a pattern, a vision, on one level or multiple levels within your being. These levels can and do exist as influences from the past in this or previous incarnations, and influences which you have as memories from other realms. These are the patterns from whence you can choose, or you can take the best from these and, because you have free will, you can create anew. You can look upon the raw material, just as a craftsperson. In your case, it shall be life, itself ... the entities whom you shall interact with in daily experience, all of the substance, whether this be structures or mechanical contrivances or wood carvings or stone, paper, whatever, these are all tools, raw materials. If you see them as such, you empower yourself.

Instead of seeing self as being the focal point of influence of all things external from self, reverse this. See yourself as the focal point of influence on all that is about you. Knoweth thou not the difference between a word of loving encouragement and one of criticism? Certainly. Then, choose. And choose creatively. Build a new pattern, a new blueprint, to encourage others. Look for ways to see the beauty and not the flaws. Find paths that lead you to seeing all this within self, for, in order to form outwardly a perfect pattern, and to build and create in an ideal of perfection of spirit at the highest level, must this not come from a source which has claimed it?

You are creating ... in your thoughts, in your words, in your deeds.

July 10

Some entities ask about a lifetime, and they like to know things about, who were they, what was their name, what did they do, were they related to or have interactions with anyone they know in the current life, was their son or daughter or wife or mother or father or aunt or uncle present and, if so, to what capacity?

Do you ever hear them ask, "Did I learn to love myself and forgive myself, so that I could love and forgive others?"

Did I learn to love myself and forgive myself, so that I could love and forgive others?

July 11

There shall always be those who are enhungered until the Earth has reached its point of growth wherein the nourishment cometh from God and God, alone. Where one seeks to infill themselves with the bounty of the material, these cannot long endure in the sense of the eternal balance of the forces of truth, for, even the illusion of the most powerful force must one day be recognized as an illusion.

It could be interpreted as having a lack of heart to say such as, those souls who hunger and depart their physical bodies have chosen to so do. We would quickly add that you have chosen to be in the Earth with them, and to know of it.

You have asked, how may we help? You can first begin to tip the scales of balance, that the positive power in the Earth becomes the greater, and that the veils of illusion and separateness and the thought-form of habit can be seen and known for what they are. If you wish to help them, then do what you know to do.

Think on these things, as well: On the next Earth day after you have heard these words, do not have a thought of hostility, of anger, of remorse or sadness, without taking hold of it immediately and claiming your right of direction, of control, and transforming it into a power of God. If you do that, you have helped them, for, they cannot be in hunger if there is nothing about them but plenty. See? You live within a thought-form agreed upon by a greater number of souls. You are those who have the power to change that thought-form.

You are those who have the power to change the thought-form agreed upon by a greater number of souls.

July 12

If one understands these guidances from God, His covenant with thee, perhaps His map of return to oneness with Him, or, if ye will, His Commandments, then one understands the Universal Laws, and one understands the working of that force called karma, and one knows these to be an aspect of our Father's grace

As man holds those that are the heritage in endearment, they hold an aspect of God in reverence, for God has permitted there to be His Grace in order that thou shall be born of man and, yet, be His, and born of woman and, yet, be eternal ... that there is, in the union of man and woman, the symbolic union of those poles, or polarities, which indicate to you at the onset of birth the need to unite the kingdom within and that which is without.

The union of man and woman is symbolic at birth: the need to unite the kingdom within and that which is without.

July 13

If thee do not respond to the need of another, art thou damned? Likely so, for, self will judge based upon the Law. Is this the damnation spoken of by so many? No, it is not.

By choosing to judge self, you create the opportunity for karma to take place. This is merely the opportunity to experience again some event, some activity, which shall allow for the understanding to create grace. It is the grace, then, that is the bread of our Father's Word, and it is that of which thee will nourish self and emerge pure.

By choosing to judge self, you create the opportunity for karma to take place.

July 14

Ultimately, every petal of a flower will look to its center. It will look to its point of contact with the total flower for its nourishment, for its support, and so forth.

Even in the Earth, when it might seem to be the darkest hour, there is always that support from the Center of all existence. And the darkness will always give way to light in its season and in accordance with the will and purposes of those souls involved.

Ultimately, every petal of a flower will look to its center for its nourishment.

July 15

Suggesting that entities release other entities is something that should be done all through their life, not just at the moment of departure.

To love an entity is not to hold them, to bind them, to cling to them. It's to cherish and nurture them, openly, in the palm of your outstretched hand. If you admired a lovely songbird in a flowering bush just in front of you, would you think of reaching out and grasping it and clutching it in your hand because you loved its presence and its song so much that you didn't want to let it go? That's the whole issue there. If you hold it a bit too long, you'll harm it, you'll damage it. You'll prevent it from being the thing of beauty that you loved in the first place. See?

To love an entity is not to hold them, to bind them, to cling to them. It's to cherish and nurture them, openly.

July 16

There are those of the faithful who come unto the temple so oft and offer the chapter and verse as has been written, and do so fluently. And there are those of the faithful who are out and about in the fields of life, sowing seed, nurturing it, and bringing in the harvest to those who have a need of it.

It is difficult indeed, if possible, for we here to assess, this one is the greater than the other, for, who can say what the harvest is, indeed, except that one knows within they have done that which they know to do. They have given that which they have to give and, in this manner, are they to be gathered up to walk with He who is our Brother.

Seek ye not, then, that which is the letter and verse but, rather, that which is alive within it.

Seek ye not, then, that which is the letter and verse but, rather, that which is alive within it.

July 17

Be not shy at that which seeks from the Father but, just as has been given by the Christ, do these things and the greater will come.

Listen and you will hear. Look and you will see.

Be the greater that you know to be, and more will be given than you can surmise. Open your heart to be that which you believe is possible and, then, open it greater.

Open your heart to be that which you believe is possible and, then, open it greater.

July 18

As these energies, forces, and intentions rise up, offer peace for those who have lost their way or know not to seek that which is within them.

Offer peace for those who have lost their way or know not to seek that which is within them.

July 19

Isn't it curious how one reality can so quickly and easily give way to another? The reality of a thought you hold in heart or mind can, in the next moment, be whisked away, and another comes to take it's place.

But, when you hold an intention and you believe unto that intention in the attitude of a child of God – in other words, with faith and joyful expectancy – then, this becomes the enduring reality. Prayer offered from such a position bears the power of a child of God.

Nonetheless, be not attached to the outcome, for, the outcome can be that which misleads. It is not in the outcome that is manifest, but in that power which surrounds it that can create.

The power of prayer does not vanquish. It blesses. It nourishes. It brings light to the darkness. Thus, dis-ease, which is so oft the darkness of illusion or the error of a choice made from poor reflection or whatnot, then, the power of the prayer brings light to this and the forgiveness as is of God. Then, the dis-ease no longer has reality, and the reality which is yours to give becomes predominant.

That is healing, see?

Prayer offered from a position of faith and joyful expectancy bears the power of a child of God.

July 20

For the Emotion: These then can effect the emotive, the subliminal influences, for, the sensitivity to the glandular centers may come under some increased stimulus. So it is good to exercise the energy centers – charkas, the glandular centers – with some exercise that stimulates the spinal on a regular schedule, if not daily. These will help to bring the glandular centers into a more gradual shift.

For the Mind: We would ensure that the footwear (strange as it might seem to some) is very good, supporting good postural integration. This can help to keep a state of ease in the body, mind, and spirit all throughout the forthcoming changes.

For the Spirit: Much more dependency needs to be upon that which is of spirit ... truth, honor, and such. Here we would point to the relationship between self and that which is believed, as in faith, that those passages through times of challenge can be made with greater and greater ease, for, the accomplishment of this, then, determines the benefits that can come on the "other side of these events."

For the Body: All of these things can be enhanced by providing the body those trace elements as are to fuel the body's combustive nature and the glandular centers to keep it in a state of good ease. See?

———

Footwear that is supporting good postural integration can help to keep a state of ease in the body, mind, and spirit.

July 21

That time cometh near when He will call you. Be at the ready, that you can answer.

That time cometh near when He will call you. Be at the ready, that you can answer.

July 22

Those who will stand to the forefront will stand in the greatest fires of purification, for, the forces which oppose have their right to test thee.

Just so as the Father will always provide thee with what is needed, He will also permit thee to strengthen thyself against the opposition to the Light, for, it is better, you see, that the gradual strengthening occurs before the greater testing shall come before thee.

So, in all that has transpired, learn from this. Be loving and gentle to self and to others and work upon patience. This is much needed now and will be needed even moreso in the future.

Those who will stand to the forefront will stand in the greatest fires of purification, so, be gentle and loving to self.

July 23

In the temples of old, there was often called that time of prayer and that time of honor in this way or that.

These temples are now truly being awakened within each of you. Think of them not as in a distant place called the Holy Land. Think of them, now, as that Holy place within, that these are the "holy lands" to be looked upon from whence shall be born the opening of the way for the Promise. As you look unto self for this, the temple within, then, the honor and the Word can be made manifest, and the resonance of the Word can be heard by all.

Be that, then, and know the glory of the Father, His spirit eternal, within you.

The temples of old are now being awakened within each of you, that the honor and the Word can be made manifest.

July 24

The most dynamic, the most powerful, force in the Earth is the Children of God, and the Spirit of God is the foundation.

What you are willing to put into your life, what you contribute as an individual in terms of mass-mind thought, this is a part of the directive control that you have over the healing fields.

The most dynamic, the most powerful, force in the Earth is the Children of God, and the Spirit of God is the foundation.

July 25

The Spirit called Christ is the eternal essence of the children of God. It is the Light, the presence of life, itself, and it is eternal. It is the source of truth. It is the reservoir of omnipotent power, and nothing is beyond its potential. Yet, in the Earth, so many would have it seem that only the man called Jesus bears this gift from God and, yet, in His own words and teachings did He say different than this.

How could our Master say to you, to all of us, that all these things and greater shall ye do if He did not know that that within Him is also within all others? For, it is, as He demonstrated, this Christ Spirit which doeth the work, not the hands physical, not the mind of matter, nor any such which is merely the momentary focus of consciousness, called finiteness.

The Spirit called Christ is the eternal essence of the children of God.

July 26

Mass-thought can be an opportunity, for, energy is energy. If you are properly upon your ideal, purposes, and goals, then, you will find that this is simply so much more available energy. The caution here, again, is to occasionally take time to rebalance and stabilize yourself with the natural forces to avoid possible excessive rapidity in your growth or your pursuit of activities, as the Master would replenish and rebalance Himself in the mountains or the wilderness, as called. See?

Mass-thought can be an opportunity, for, energy is energy. If you are properly upon your ideal, purposes, and goals.

July 27

As one seeks to build their will, it is good to *know* the will, to know the joys, the happiness of self. If one denies the happiness and goals, they are denying an integral part of their own being.

Will is a force which can be extremely useful as a tool in service to God, to self, and of course, to others, for, if a work is God's work, it is a work for all. As one builds a will and has knowledge of their will, there must be the recognition that cooperation and harmony must be considered, and the Laws of God. A will is a force. It is not a purpose, as such. It is not necessarily a goal. A will is a tool that is fashioned out of the knowledge of self. The knowledge of self is accomplished by knowing the ideal, the purposes, and goals. See?

The magnetizing of self is the building of a thought-form, pure and simple, and that is, simply, to envision and to believe unto something so strongly that it is a magnetic force surrounding thee and around that object or objective. Will is that which prepares a pathway towards this or that, but, moreover, unto a way of life. Will is the part of self which is the sword of truth. Will can sever the clouds of darkness and part them. Will is that which is associated with the highest ideal when used properly. When misused there is likely the need to examine the Laws of God, for, they are potentially, if not certainly, being violated. To build a good will learn more about self. See?

Will is the part of self which is the sword of truth. Will can sever the clouds of darkness and part them.

July 28

When one seeks to be a more effective channel of blessing or seeks to serve as a disciple of God, there must be the understanding that all entities are offered this same opportunity and this work. Knowing that all God's children are equally blessed, then, recognizing that self, knowing and hearing this call and, thusly, accepting same, is the great honor to self and to the joy in these realms.

Knowing, further, that God is not without His great state of grace, then, know that that state of grace is the greatest tool that thee have with which to work. When one applies grace for another, when one looks to another entity and uses the Law of Grace to forgive and to transform that entity from a state of limited sight into one of joy and hope, then, that is the gain to thee as the giver of the state of humbleness.

In order to be humble, one must be willing to allow their self to accept that there will not be loss through humbleness but, rather, the gain. If you seek to develop humbleness, then, seek to bring joy to others. For, seeing joy in others where it was not is one of the greatest tools one can use to develop that which ye call humbleness. See?

Grace is the greatest tool that thee have with which to work.

July 29

Humbleness does not mean that you would relinquish your state of joy and your acceptance of your own blessings as a child of God. Humbleness is to know these things and, in spite of that knowledge, to continue on in service.

As one sees the greatness and the unlimited power of self as a living expression of God, therein, at that point lies one of the greater struggles in the evolvement of self, for, in knowing the power, the temptation is present to use it only for the gain of self and only for the edification and illumination of self.

In seeing the unlimited power of self as an expression of God lies one of the greater struggles in the evolvement of self.

July 30

As you consider your thoughts, then, consider that
attitudes and emotions are generally the substances from
which thoughts build.
Just so, then, as ye would think, there is the trigger or
stimuli to the emotional centers, which are very reactive or
very responsive to the thought-form and do cause a change, a
secretion from the glandular centers of the body.

Attitudes and emotions are generally the substances from
which thoughts build.

July 31

Do balance self each Earth day, that the physical, mental, and spiritual are treated in a harmonious state.

Do not relinquish the consciousness of one for the consciousness of another, for, thee must understand that the presence of the body physical in the Earth is a glorious and beautiful gift and opportunity. To relinquish it totally for a spiritual consciousness is similar to a workman casting off his tools to hold to the vision of that which he might build with them. Thee must retain all. Thee must maintain contact and excellence with thy tools, which is, in this instance, the body and mental awareness physical.

The presence of the body physical in the Earth is a glorious and beautiful gift and opportunity.

August 1

The purpose of guides is to acquaint you with the God within. Angels who guide ofttimes will bring you a word or two from the Father. The first step and the most important is the willingness to listen. Do not miss, one day of your life, the joyousness of hearing and knowing He is one with thee.

Do not miss, one day of your life, the joyousness of hearing and knowing He is one with thee.

August 2

Begin where you are with what you have, and that is the power of your prayer, your thoughts, and your meditations.

Begin where you are with what you have, and that is the power of your prayer, your thoughts, and your meditations.

August 3

The point is simply this, again: It's not so much what you do, but what you hold in your heart and mind.

If you call your spirit, your spirit is answering. But, then, if you go off into life and pick up the mantle of habit, and act as though your spirit hasn't answered you, then, you'll have to pause and do whatever ... whether that's to pray, using prayer beads, or any such, whatever it takes, to reopen yourself to know it.

It's not so much what you do, but what you hold in your heart and mind.

August 4

If you choose a path and open self with an intent to be one with all that is within you and, if you choose to set aside that which thou knoweth limits – even so as is familiar, comfortable, and perhaps even loved – then can you claim, as given in the works called the Course In Oneness, the potential to move into that state of righteousness, which clears the sight, opens the way, and enables you to see, not only through the eyes, but to create a conduit through which the healing intent can flow.

Open self with an intent to be one with all that is within you and you choose to set aside that which thou knoweth limits.

August 5

Prayer is an empowerment. It is that which goes forth and surrounds the recipient, in effect, in a sphere of light. The degree to which they are willing in that moment to receive same, truly willing, and to release that which was familiar, even though it may be a state of dis-ease ... All of this, collectively, determines the immediacy, or lack thereof, of the result of the prayer.

Prayer is an empowerment. It is that which goes forth and surrounds the recipient, in effect, in a sphere of light.

August 6

Journeys in the Earth, dear friends, are blessings. Indeed, these blessings are sought after by many.

Journeys in the Earth, dear friends, are blessings. Indeed, these blessings are sought after by many.

August 7

In those times [of Jesus], even in the confrontation of what could be called non-accomplishment, failure, there was not the disappointment but, rather, wonder and lightness at finding that this path did not function the way it was anticipated. It was considered a discovery, an enlightenment, and something to build upon, not held personally or emotionally. For, so doing, greatly limits self and prevents the expression of that joy, which is the nature of your spirit and of course, your soul.

Never judge self by the outcome in the Earth. For the Earth is not always respectful of the spirit and love of those striving to serve. The return of the love and joy of service comes from within self, from the wellspring within and from that Light that cometh to thee as you give these on the part of those whom were served and those you encounter. Be cautious not to judge your own creations where this is in word, deed or a literal creative work based upon the actions or reactions or non-reactions of others and disappointments in the past. What could be called betrayal is merely a discovery. It is not intended to be a burden. See? Be lighthearted with self and the same with life. See life as a wondrous opportunity for discovery. See? Ready here.

The Earth is not always respectful of the spirit and love of those striving to serve.

August 8

To sustain a state of consciousness is to love it, and
believe it above all else.

The Master, as Jesus, never held a doubt within Himself
that He was and is the Son of God, that He and the Father
are One. If you seek to make self into something that you
believe in, that is worthy, that you know will contribute to
your accomplishment of your ideal, then, do as He, just in
that manner: Love it, believe in it, nourish it, as though it
were a child given to you from God that lives within you
eternally.

To sustain a state of consciousness is to love it, and
believe it above all else.

August 9

Do align self in meditation and select those environments which will promote for the greater balance for the physical body. These should include as near as possible consistent environment for meditation. (This does not apply for all, for, some are at varying levels of ability to accept or balance body, mind, and spirit.)

We find greater achievements would be made when the body aligns itself north-south, facing north. This should include the entity having some period of meditation which includes the infilling of spirit or the indwelling of knowledge in this way.

Do have a prayerful attitude for some fifteen or twenty minutes before meditation, very consciously divesting self of previous thought.

Do keep the body and thy personage as cleanly as possible, for, after all, this is God's temple and keep it in such reverence.

Do find entities of like mind or else meditate alone.

Do find that, as the light and the sound about thee do enhance the ability to perceive, try to make these consistent and never face directly electrical lights, as their vibrations or emanations can diffuse the thought. ... acceptable to the overhead or to the rear, but not to the front. See?

For greater acheivement (for some), in meditation, align self north-south, facing north, and never face electrical lights.

August 10

The greater is your honor and love for the self that is you as a child of God, the greater shall you receive honor and love from those who are now moving into the Earth as a realm of expression.

The greater you honor self as a child of God, the greater shall you receive honor from those now moving into the Earth.

August 11

The glory of God is never distant. It is an arm's length away. It is that which you can find within and without.

But, as you reach forth in the manner as you would with an arm, that very action is an intent, and the intent has been acted upon.

The glory of God is never distant. It is an arm's length away.

August 12

Call forth this then:

"I am [Name], son/daughter of God. From this moment forward, I honor my heritage and I claim this in all that I am and do. I release myself from any illusions of guilt or debt or burden, as I release others from any sense of guilt or debt or burden. I grant all others the right of freedom and, thus, in return, I claim and accept my freedom. Whatsoe'r another's choice may be is theirs to do. My choice is mine to do and, as I imbue my choice to be one with my intent and act upon this, then, I emerge in the truth of who I am, and that truth is an eternal child of God, honoring the precepts, the beliefs, the choices of others wheresoever I might journey, but affirming that I am never bound by these. When one comes to me who wishes to impose anything upon me, I do not dispute this with them, neither do I seek to counterpoint it. But, I am free, and I choose my intent and act upon it.

"It is as the wind blowing through the trees ... a gentle breeze that passes by, but it cannot linger, for, I give it no home, no shelter. I give it honor and the peace of God, that it may journey and, as it chooses, act."

I am a child of God. From this moment forward, I honor my heritage and I claim this in all that I am and do.

August 13

Now we stand at the threshold, all of us. Let us rejoice and celebrate one another. Let us open to the completeness of our eternal nature, cherishing the beauty of that uniqueness as God gives as life to us eternally, and let us do as the Christ has promised: all these things and greater. Let us be in our awareness that which we are, brothers and sisters, seeing no separateness, seeing nothing that limits, seeing that which is for what it is: choices of journeys, choices of experiences, choices of good intentions to serve, but never separately.

"If a man comes along a dusty path and finds a child weeping in Sudan and bends to take the hem of his garment to wipe the child's face, I wipe that child's face with him. If a good medical person seeks to mend a wound by dim candle-light in a war-ravaged building in Syria, I tend that wound with him."

So, who is it that is with you, tending that wound with that good medical worker. Your hand upon the good physician's is the hand of the Christ. Your love for this man and the wounded one is the love of the Christ. Your offering of healing grace to the wounded one is the offering of the Christ. Your words of comfort to the wounded one are the words spoken by the Christ. You and the good medical worker, are the Christ, seeking to bring comfort to one in need.

Say these things in a manner as suits you, and believe them. That is the meaning of no separateness.

Let us rejoice and celebrate one another, brothers and sisters, seeing no separateness.

August 14

One should always work for that of a harmony within self as well as with others. Should develop a strengthening of the spiritual with the mental, as well, then, manifesting same in the physical. Do find that your purpose, just so as in past, is still the same ... to perfect and implement the concept that the Christ Spirit is universal throughout all souls and all space/time. Finding this as a realization within self will help thee, then, to give this unto others.

Purposes and tasks should be to give and share joy to others, to be understanding and forgiving, and to recognize the difference between souls who are seeking and souls who are wanting.

Do develop the attitude toward the Earth plane that this is a temporary place for thee to dwell, and that service to others is service to self, and that so, then, such service should be given and become a part of that constant way ... certainly without the detriment to self, for loving self is as important as loving thy neighbor.

Build within self an awareness of that temple, which is that temple wherein God dwells. And do go forward in this life with the concept that God is to the right and left of thee, as thou art a part of Same. See?

Go forward in this life with the concept that God is to the right and left of thee, as thou art a part of Same.

August 15

For, remember: you cannot do a work in God's name without God blessing yourself equally to your intent. So, as you lift up another, you lift up self. As you inspire and strengthen, by kind words and deeds, another's resolve in the Earth, you have done so unto yourself.

You cannot do a work in God's name without God blessing yourself equally.

August 16

The body is all interrelated, not just a physical body controlled distantly by the thought, by the spiritual pattern. The separateness of the spiritual, mental, and physical is only for the purpose of reference and discussion. There is, in effect, only one being, and that is a spiritual being.

This spiritual force, then, projects itself to be the life-form and to assemble, in accordance with its vibrational frequency, the necessary elements to form the physical body. Witness, then, when the spirit leaves the body, the molecular structure of those elements begins almost immediately, or within three or so Earth days, to disperse itself, returning to the source which most clearly vibrates in harmony with its own individual particle nature. You see? Hence, the term, ashes to ashes, dust to dust. Like to like. See?

So the will of the entity is important here. The joy of the spirit, and the clear and pronounced ability to know self to be eternal, is a major aspect in the promotion of healing in any body physical.

Joy of the spirit, and the clear ability to know self to be eternal, is a major aspect in the healing in any body physical.

August 17

Were each soul to be tempered identically, we should believe that the glory of God would be less illuminated in the eyes of these beholders, for, they would all see Him the same. The true beauty and luminosity (we humbly submit) might well be thought of as being as infinite and as wondrous as it truly is *because* there are as many different, if not infinite, eyes, minds, and spirits who perceive same.

The quality of life in the Earth could well be measured in a similar way: That, as there are as many different viewpoints and perspectives, these, in a better environment of hopefulness, of joy and understanding, could well bring about a realm of total harmony, an Eden-like garden, wherein all know and love the uniqueness of others, that no one soul would seek to conquer or to overcome or dominate. For, they would know that, by so doing, they would diminish just that much more of their own potential because of the deterrent to the flow of energy, the very life force, to their realm's potential.

Many different viewpoints in an environment of joy and understanding could bring about a realm of harmony, Eden-like.

August 18

Be thou ever true to self. Reach back to know self and to claim that.

Open the way. Make it passable, that the sum of self can bring forth the evolution of self into what can be … not mysterious, not requiring rote, or drudgery, or dogma, but only the casting off of that which would limit and the claiming of that which sets self free.

Look about your life as though it were a house, just like in dream symbology, and see … Are things arranged within the house of life by choice, or by happenstance? Are the aspects, which may appear as articles in the house, your choosing, or did someone else or something else put them there?

Claim the power and the right and choose. Rearrange. Alter it. Place upon the stoop that which is not desired any longer. Let someone else who might be served by it gather it up as they pass by.

The sweetness of Our Lord is constantly offered to you just as you in past offered your sweetness to Him.

Be thou ever true to self.

August 19

When you conclude this lifetime, it is like setting aside a well-worn, used coat or garment. You have become so familiar and so much a part of it that it symbolizes all that you are. Perhaps, only when you remove it and set it aside, do you fully recognize who and what you are. Your potential is limited only to the degree that you allow it to be. If you believe in yourself and know that the presence of God within is not simply words, not an empty promise, but a literal fact and, then, you live your life evidencing that fact as a way of thinking and a way of acting, you will have transcended one of the major lessons and accomplishments of this life.

You are encouraged to think much more broadly, much more all-inclusively, of yourself as being one with all things. The degree to which that oneness can be seen and demonstrated depends upon self.

Your potential is limited only to the degree that you allow it to be.

August 20

Changes and challenges seem to be bedfellows in the Earth. With change, the reluctance of those who are familiar with certain patterns and certain methodologies will create challenges as the new strives to bring its light, thrusting fingers of hope, seeds for the future promise, into the old ways. Those who wish to hold the old may resist.

So, as it is within and above, so shall it be, then, in the Earth, as well. All who can hear shall hear, and those who can see shall witness the passing of these old ways.

From the old, there will always come the foundational building blocks of the future. If these are troubled, it is that which shall be shall remain for all of time to come in the heritage or future heritage of the Earth. Lest this not be so, then, look at yourselves daily to see, what is being thought, what actions are being taken, what words are being spoken ... Are they reactionary to the conditioning activities from the past, or are they openly responsive to the stimulus and opportunity of the future?

Changes and challenges seem to be bedfellows in the Earth. Those who wish to hold the old may resist.

August 21

The "forces of destruction," or the forces of opposition, are creations of consciousness in Earth, or, in the minds called human or finite.

Those minds which are unlimited or infinite have no sense of the description of destruction. A force of God cannot de-struct or de-structure that which is created of God. There is naught which can do this.

The "forces of destruction" or the forces of opposition are creations of the minds called human or finite.

August 22

In the journey called life in Earth, there are many facets to be explored. Many of these facets can be found outwardly and have definition, have form, have parameters, and a somewhat universal understanding. In example here, we could point to a tree and say most all in the Earth would know that a tree is a tree and understand its definition.

The great gift that is being offered to those of you who are seeking now is to understand beyond mere definition, though this has great value and is a part of the journey, itself ... but to understand that which has not a rigid or summarily agreed-upon definition by the universality of consciousness in the Earth. So often, this is found only by a journey within.

The inward journey, or, as called, the great passageway, is an eternal potential for all of you.

The inward journey, or, as called, the great passageway, is an eternal potential for all of you.

August 23

The power of God within you is unlimited. You are the limiting force.

The power of God within you is unlimited. You are the limiting force.

August 24

Recognize who you are, accepting yourself, knowing yourself, and being faithful unto what you believe. Distill all of that down and call it, quite simply, purity. It is not piety. It is purity.

When you are in a pure consciousness of yourself, you have recognized your emotions, you have seen and examined whatsoe'er may be within you as fears or doubts, anger, love, joy, whate'er is present, and you have a purity of consciousness or acceptance of this. Then, no matter how dense the sphere might be between thee and Universal Consciousness, you can pass through it as though nothing existed. The purer and more in harmony you become, the further you can reach until, ultimately, what we've called the veil of darkness can be transcended.

You create a pathway, then, along which your soul-consciousness moves to and fro from what we would call God consciousness or Universal Consciousness and the finite awareness of your expression in the Earth. It is through such a mechanism that we are now communicating with you. You refer to it as the Channel, but the Source is universal. If you stop short of the Source, you would be stopping short of the potential. Thus, the further and more pure you are able to go with that pursuit, the greater is the potential, the more unlimited is the nature.

The more in harmony you become, the further you can reach until, the veil of darkness can be transcended.

August 25

Your spirits are bright. You search for something that you believe will be the answer, be the key, and that is good and we are joyful to assist; but all that you seek is always within you. We are joyful to work with you to assist you, to lift you up when you fall, to bring light when you are in darkness, and to celebrate whatever choice you make; but it is you who doeth the work, for, the Father is within you.

If you feel aright with a certain choice, then, hold that for a time. Perhaps dwell on it overnight and ask God to guide. Then, if it is still aright, choose. But never should there be the lamenting of that which appears in the measure of Earth as a wrong choice, for, it is an opportunity to gain perspective, wisdom, and understanding.

Never should there be the lamenting of that which appears to be a wrong choice. For, it is an opportunity to gain.

August 26

As you ponder whether or not your work might be, in truth, a gift or a blessing, labor not long over this, but look at your intent. For, the Law of Just Intent says that as thou give it according to that which you know to be the highest and best, then this shall be what shall manifest thereafter.

Where is the fault if the just intent is to give a gift of brilliance, beauty, to those who would have it?

The Law of Just Intent: As you give according to what you know to be the highest and best, this is what shall manifest.

August 27

Would do well to endow self with greater time for that meditative practice which would enable the greater realization and consummation of unison of spirit and mind. It is suggested strongly that this is particularly important during these times when stress upon the Earth plane mass-mind becomes so prevalent.

Do manifest this as an opportunity to receive the eternal being and to have knowledge and wisdom to use same towards the betterment of all mankind.

Be a contributing factor in each action and deed, and think of the interaction that minds do have, regardless of the spoken word. Realize that, as your thoughts emanate, so does an energy-pattern practice and manifest what your thoughts do create. Just as one sends sound from the verbal muscular chords of the throat or larynx, so does the mind emanate vibrations much similar and akin to same.

Realize that, as your thoughts emanate, so does an energy pattern manifest your thoughts.

August 28

In order to pass from one realm of consciousness to that which lies beyond – to ascend, so to say, or to move into the Light (as it is so often called in the Earth) – one must meet that which has been the journey being left behind.

One must meet that which has been the journey being left behind.

August 29

There are moments here and there that are special for you, special in the sense that these are pauses in your journey through life where prayers for you have been placed long ago by others who have known and loved you afar. In these special moments – as you would feel them with a subtlety, with a flush of energy, with the twinkle of light in another's eye not known to you, a stranger passing by – pause, then, and be the recipient of that blessing which has been placed here along your pathway by dear brethren, brothers and sisters, who have loved you from afar and who love you even now.

As you look about and see the journeys of others, some whom you know and others not, pause and send forth a prayer to await them on *their* journey. That, when they pause, it can surround them and bless them, that they will know their path is not preordained, mandated, but one flush with choices, as a spring tree flushes with blossoms of color.

Seek ye, then, that moment of peace and, as you do, recognize and affirm we are with you ... we who have walked with you in past, and who are here walking with you unseen, perhaps, in your presence.

Prayers for you have been placed along your journey through life long ago by others who have loved you from afar.

August 30

You are that power expressed of God in the realm in which you dwell, called Earth.

You are that power expressed of God in the realm in which you dwell, called Earth.

August 31

If a man walketh in the darkness of night and can see not his way, and one comes with a light in hand, which is the greater? The light, itself, or the man's intent who brings it? It is in the darkness that one finds the light and, in the light, that one finds the darkness. It is not measured in the denominations or categorization of emotion in the Earth. It is found in that center of life within you, and it is this that is the greatest treasure that you have to give. And it is eternal.

It is in the darkness that one finds the light and, in the light, that one finds the darkness.

September 1

So many of you who have had those loved ones on the Earth plane depart from your side have pondered, indeed, why this one should leave at a particular time. It is not what you would call accidental or random selection. It is, rather, that these souls, in the majority of cases, have completed their task for that lifetime and, therefore, have no further need of that body nor its true confining nature. Yes, there are sorrows that are felt. Not for the loss of that physical body, but sorrows that there cannot be the continuation of assistance to others in the Earth plane in physical body.

The use of prayer is so very important here, dear friends. Prayer is a form of thought and energy that is not restricted to any particular level, realm or sphere. It can transcend the densest matter and rise to the most purified levels. Very little else, save those of high levels of acceptance of God, can accomplish this. Prayer is a form of God's Grace in action. In the trueness of this, it is the living God which is permitted, through thy works and these, to be manifested on behalf of thee and others.

Prayer is a form of God's Grace in action. It is the living God permitted, through these works, to be manifested.

September 2

Karma is neither bad nor good; it simply exists. It is the force of being that continues to urge and prod you towards the balancing with events past and those planned for future. It can be placed aside for a period of time, but it must be understood within thy being.

It does not mean that, for a karmic action in a past lifetime, one must live an entire lifetime, for, time is not of a significance that you purport it to be on your plane. It is, rather, that you progress in one, two, or twenty lifetimes until *your* mind and heart are merged in the understanding of the completeness of that karmic action. Once this is accomplished – and it may be so in one day's existence or one hundred thousand days ... your choice, you see – then the karmic pattern is balanced and you will choose to go on.

Karmic pattern can be balanced in one day's existence or one hundred thousand days ... your choice, you see.

September 3

In the canine, there can be found qualities that are
God-like ... the capacity for inestimable forgiveness,
patience, love, and faithfulness, and qualities which endear
these creatures to receive just so what they give, and a great
deal more. The bond which is formed between the individual,
called the owner, and the canine is beyond expression in
mere words or sentences or paragraphs, for, one has only but
to look into the eyes of one of these creatures to see them
looking back, radiating something which, again, words cannot
embrace.

There can be those, who have no warmth in their heart
for such creatures, who would counter with this or that and,
unto these, we would simply offer in humbleness, you cannot
know of such a bond, such a warmth and love and companionship until you open yourself in a single moment to
communicate same with one of them.

It is written in many great works that to love God is to
love all of creation, and that the reflection of one's love in
such shall abundantly flow in return to one willing to give.
Few, if any, categories of creation such as the canine so
marvelously and magnificently demonstrate same.

In the canine are qualities that are God-like ... the capacity
for inestimable forgiveness, patience, love, and faithfulness.

September 4

Learn this much from the felines: They are capable of giving tremendous quantities of love. They can protect, nurture, and guide. When they know the point that their presence may inhibit or limit, without a moment's hesitation, they will turn around and depart. You've seen this as they train and love and care for their own offspring, haven't you? When they know the time is proper for them to go forward for other experiences, it's as though they have never known that creature. They simply turn about. See?

The feline consciousness is capable of reaching into several realms simultaneously. They are capable of perception in multiple realms. Their progression is on a multiple level. Their work with you in the Earth plane is to generally uplift your spirit, to move your consciousness, that you can encompass multiple realms, as well. They are the light which is found in your shadow. They are the illumination which occurs with insight.

Their involvement in the Earth plane is largely to help, to be an adjunct to the works of mankind. The entry into the Earth plane in form, in physical form, is largely under the dominion of mankind, as it is with all other kingdoms else than the souls themselves.

The feline's work is to generally uplift your spirit, to move your consciousness, that you can encompass multiple realms.

September 5

The nature of the Earth is such that it acts as a veil, a partition, which is capable of preserving and sustaining the integrity of the desires and thought-forms of the greater number of souls involved with same.

Therefore, there is some subjective result from this that impacts you. For as long as you are in the Earth, this will continue to the greater or lesser degree as relates to your willingness to participate in that thought-form in the manner or in the aspects as is expected of you.

As long as you are in the Earth, it will impact you to the degree that you are willing to participate as is expected of you.

September 6

It is spirit that doeth the work.
It is mind that conceives it.
It is emotion that gives it life
And the body, the identify, the personage of the individual
or individuals who create it as a reality.

It is spirit that doeth the work, the mind that conceives it, the
emotion that gives it life, the body that creates it as reality.

September 7

The individual in the Earth has its counterpart here in the spirit expression of individuality.

What we are attempting to convey to you is, do not believe that, beyond the Earth – into other realms and beyond, indeed, in the All – that the stunning beauty of uniqueness found in the individual is ever lost. That is the misconception of many, and certainly that which limits many.

Do not believe that, beyond the Earth, the stunning beauty of uniqueness found in the individual is ever lost.

September 8

What is peace? Is it the stepping away from that which would limit? Is it the movement into the passive, where there is naught that can trouble, nor lure thee from a sense of utter balance of ease? Is it the peace in knowing that you have journeyed as thou knoweth to do?

What is peace to you? You can define it from the Earth in your current journey. You can define it from your heart, your spirit, and on and on, and if you make a contribution to that quest, you have done much of goodness. For, the children of God have the power to create, and they create through definition, and build upon it.

What one has as an accomplishment or breakthrough, as you call it, is a gift to all. It is to this that we have encouraged, celebrate the accomplishments of your brother and sister. Lift it up in praise and thankfulness.

What one has as an accomplishment or breakthrough, as you call it, is a gift to all.

September 9

When it is asked, when it is stated with the sincerity of faith and spirit, then can it be given.

Thus, there is the connection offered, ever, to all souls, all entities ... that, as you ask it and *believe* it, it is yours.

As you ask it and *believe* it, it is yours.

September 10

How so does one judge them? Do not, for their way is their own choice. Judge only that which is the bounty of thine own joy and, as such, this will bring to thee the harvest all the moreso greater.

There is the perfect cycle that is a part of the Earth lifetime (or any expression, for that matter) and that is, as it begins so does it come unto itself again and again as circles, if you will, spiraling upwards, each time offering the participant, or the entity involved, the higher sight.

Some choose to go round and about in a concentric circle and not arise. Others actually can go "downward," but not for long. In the choice to move on upward, there is the challenge offered. Why is this? The greater is the miracle in God's name, the greater is the opposition unto it. If thou maketh those who cannot see to see, then, there will be that which opposes this, for, is there not a certain dominion over those who cannot see by those who choose to dominate? For, not seeing goes beyond the physical sight. It broadens into spectrums that divide, that separate, that seem to create illusionary barriers, that seem to provide pathways that run at cross-currents to one another and, yet, are a part of what is called the One Work. See?

The greater is the miracle in God's name, the greater is the opposition unto it.

September 11

The water of spirit is likened to a light. If you go forth and find it, and claim it, and take it within, then it will shine from you. And those who truly seek it will find that it brings them unto their thirst's fulfillment.

Not because it is you, not because you bear it, but because it is offered to them from the One God, of which you are a part. But they must seek the light, or the waters of life. You can only offer it, lest you look upon self as forcing them to drink. See?

The water of spirit is likened to a light. If you go forth, find it, and claim it, and take it within, then, it will shine from you.

September 12

The trace elements and many other such as is found in the sea kelp – and we shan't go into detail in this meeting – raises the endurance, the resilience of the body considerably, and helps the body to stay focused in the primary energy sense. In other words, it's a good preventative to ward off dis-ease. See?

Also, strengthens the body. Also, helps the blood stream in so many ways, including, for many, the oxygenation.

Trace elements as found in sea kelp raises the resilience of the body, helps ward off dis-ease, helps the blood stream.

September 13

Movement, evolution, progress, growth … All these are
indicative of the growing consciousness of the children of
God who journey there in the Earth and, of course, all of the
expressions within the Earth moves, grows, along with this
consciousness.

So it is that we find thou art at such a point of considerable re-growth and awakening. It is good cause to be of glad
heart, for, in the awakening, comes the realization that thou
art, indeed, His eternal child.

It is a very good time to say to self, "I shall take these
things unto myself and awaken the presence of the Father
within to the greater. So doing, I shall know that, in all that I
am about, He is with me."

Be of good cheer in these times and celebrate, regardless
of what lies without, regardless of that which seems to call to
thee, Come here in this shadow of doubt or limitation.

Stay true to that course that is the light of the Father
within. The culmination will be the completion of the entry
of the Light, which will commence the Call, the awakening. It
will also be the point at which will be the peak of reaction in
hearts, minds, and, perhaps, in and about the Earth, itself.

At the peak of reaction about the Earth, the completion of
the entry of the Light will commence the Call, the awakening.

September 14

The final shift is just this: to attain the fullness of one's being as a complete child of God, as a full manifestation of the journey. It is likened unto that in nature, for, all things bring forth the fruit, the seed, after their own kind. At this point they are at their fullest ... before the seed is given.

It is a time for you to consider, "Where are the references for my peace? Are they without or within?"

Where are the references for my peace? Are they without or within?

September 15

There is not that which is created or which can occur which is not in the knowledge of God before its occurrence. There is naught that which can be predicated as an opportunity, which is not known by the individual soul involved (or souls, as is appropriate) at some level of their being beforehand. All events, all activities, offer the entities involved a choice. There may be given, in certain instances, such intensity of event (by the measure of the Earth) so as to give rise to doubt of this, but, as one can move further and further away from the event, the perspective becomes more in order and the event, ultimately, will fall into a harmonious place upon the pathway which that soul travels.

So, in the sense of your question, do accidents occur, from the eternal sense, no, they do not. From the finite, it is possible, to the extent that the purposes are so removed from the consciousness that the gain is lost to the consciousness, on occasion, even after movement from the Earth has been completed and only after movement has been through successive spheres of consciousness does the purpose become clear or understandable. Yet, there are souls who know instantly the purpose ... perhaps the karmic opportunity, or the contribution which they as an individual soul can make to the growth of the oversoul, the greater soul consciousness, of the entities involved in that dimension or sphere.

So, accidents, in truth, do not occur.

Do accidents occur? From the eternal sense, no, they do not.

September 16

As a soul entered an incarnation and then departed, there were, of course, aftereffects ... memories, patterns which had been engaged in, which remained with that soul. Some, so powerful, so intensely focused upon by the soul itself, that the soul became "limited," using the word to give you the reference back to the soul's purest state of consciousness that would have followed their awakening as a Child of God. So the journey became one now conditioned by the just-previous lifetime.

These souls, because they could not, due to the "limitations," the fixation upon the events just previous, could not rise to the full extent of their soul's light or true potential. So, it was discovered that this could be a pattern, a cumulative one, which could take souls deeper and deeper into finiteness, losing, in essence, most all practical association with their true potential as children of God. Thus, other souls who had not lost their consciousness came forward to assist. These souls became unseen companions, oft referred to in the Earth as guides, teachers, angels, and such.

As a soul entered an incarnation and departed, there were aftereffects, patterns, which remained with that soul.

September 17

Following the just previous commentary with an example soul, let's say that this chap moved again back into the Earth, believing, in this second incarnation, that he would resolve his penchant, his unfinished business. Perhaps, to a degree, he did, but not completely, leaving some residual effect. In the process, he might have encountered some other finite aspect which, using the power of emotion, became a part of his being, as well. Hence, upon departure, another "ring of energy" (using the concentric growth rings of a tree as an example here, and only that) and the soul now had two sheaths around the brilliant inner light, which still remained in its pure and primal form. Now, even more dulled than previously, once the entity has left and is in spiritual body again, even greater is the limitation and/or burden.

So, the soul cannot reach even the height of previous between-life consciousness. Again, the soul was met and counseled. The soul struggled to free itself, yet, was always "called" back. Feelings, emotions, began to be created ... fear, anger, hatred, doubt, became the counterpoints to the soul's true nature of love and joy, of peace and compassion. It was and is known that these counterpoints are the fires of purification through which wisdom is born and the soul, surrounded by, supported by, other loving beings in its journey returned, again ... always, the soul seeking, searching, struggling to define its own uniqueness.

Counterpoints to the nature of love, joy, of peace, compassion are the fires of purification through which wisdom is born.

September 18

For the greatest of all accomplishment in the forthcoming times, do not fear, for fear builds that energy which is in opposition to harmony. Seek ye rather then that peace and joy which is your native spirit. Think of the Earth and its harmony with itself.

Fear builds that energy which is in opposition to harmony. Seek ye, rather, then, peace and joy.

September 19

The date and time will be known when He appears, whether He is first awakened within you, and you and He are one and walk together; or one who is a dancer of light in some distant land who awakens, and that is the manifestation for that one.

The greater and greater as these awaken, then will the Path be opened and passable. It cannot be given too oft here that the path of accomplishment is a sweet and gentle one to be held within yourselves and, when possible, to be shared with others of like mind, heart, and purpose. Where their spirit sings their own uniqueness to harmonize with yours, then, the greater shall be given. It is the Law, see? When you gather in this manner, in completeness, He is present ... and He is that harvest that thou seek.

Do not look, just so, for a certain day and time, but look for that which occurs within you as a dancer of light, that the awakening and He are given to thee when thou art ready. This is the Promise. And so it comes. Be of peace and good cheer. Love one another and seek naught in return. For, if you give it, the Father will give you the greater. Seek it not beyond this, for this is the best of all.

The Call has begun. He will come to you, and others of the Angelic Host, and the brothers and sisters who serve with you and who serve in the broader sense.

The Promise awakens. Seek it. Do, see, seek it.

If you give it, the Father will give you the greater. Seek it not beyond this, for this is the best of all.

September 20

There is the movement of your prayer through love, God's love, the space that exists between manifested particles, so to say. Your prayer is an energy borne on the space. It moves into the essence between the expressions that already exist and it begins to manifest.

However, the Law being perfect, it manifests in accord with same. Thus, there may not be outward manifestation, in the finite sense, as fruits for some time, even lifetimes later. See?

This is what is meant ... The gift of prayer is sent to one and surrounds them, so to say, as a living light awaiting an opportunity that the intended recipient opens themselves to receive same. If they do not, the prayer is an eternal living light and remains forever as a gift waiting to be opened.

The gift of prayer sent to one surrounds them as an eternal living light and remains forever as a gift waiting to be opened.

September 21

You are, while expressed in a finite form, nonetheless an unlimited creation of God.

You are, while expressed in a finite form, nonetheless an unlimited creation of God.

September 22

We are, each one, as the pebbles in the stream of life ...
no two precisely alike, each one a bit unique from the other.
Together, we form the bed upon which those life-giving
waters of Spirit can flow; but if we believe ourselves to be one
and the same, then, we have lost that very gift that the river of
life has intended for us. Your uniqueness must always be
thought of as precious.

Your uniqueness must always be thought of as precious.

September 23

It has been given, oft, here that, when one seeks the location in which to dwell, the better choice is that which brings the greatest joy to self, that brings that sense of oneness, belonging, and harmony within self.

Do not choose to dwell in a locale based upon that which can happen but, rather, that which is within self. Put your faith in oneness with God, and all will be well.

Do not choose to dwell in a locale based upon that which can happen but, rather, that which is within self.

September 24

If you face off into the darkness in a very dark night and entities beyond you, behind you, build a great fire and begin to dance around the flame, their shadows cast upon the darkness that you are facing will seem very great indeed; but, if you turn and face them, you will see them for what they are and, if you go beyond them, you can sit by the pure light of the fire, itself.

Do not let the shadows of other entities' dances frighten or coerce you into believing that to be greater than the eternal flame, itself. For, the flame of truth is God. Your test, your challenge in this life, is to see the flame and not the shadow. The Flame is before you in all that you do.

You can have both if you are willing to release the former ... You can participate in the drama and take from it joy, abundance, love, compassion, and give equally in kind, whether received or not; but, if you cling to the shadow, you will never be able to turn and be warmed by the fire. See?

Your test, your challenge in this life, is to see the flame and not the shadow.

September 25

   Could you shift your focus to a child of God and consider
that that child of God blocks your path?

   Have a care, and look deep within self before so doing.
For, so as you meet it out, shall it be given unto thee in
return. If thou judge, just so in that manner art thou to be
judged.

If thou judge, just so in that manner art thou to be judged.

September 26

To find the "i" in illusions is but to turn within and to recognize that this life, borne in the body, this vessel, this bowl, contains the same water retrieved from a stream. When you place it back in the stream when this life is completed, shall it be pure and sweet, or shall it carry with it debris or tainted essences that are the vestiges of unresolved events and opportunities? For, at some point, these will need to be purified if that water, which is that previous life, is ever to be completely a part of the pure flowing stream from whence it was originally taken.

To find the "i" in illusions is but to turn within.

September 27

It is written here that each soul is likened unto a voyager upon a great sea of time and space and consciousness. And that movement into different experiences here and there could well be further likened unto a vessel which takes shelter in certain various ports. And that these ports, then, when compared to a lifetime or incarnation in the Earth, could then perhaps be seen in the greater perspective of the soul's voyage. And from each point of port do ye draw that which is needed to sustain thee and to prepare for the next portion of the voyage. And that each entity, as a voyager, would do well to have a course by which they can compare and correct or make adjustment, that their destination continues to be that unto which they are heading.

And so it is, then, that each experience in the Earth is a reference point for the soul. And, through the understanding and growth which comes forth from that, the soul is granted the greater ability to adjust or do works which shall benefit and accelerate, not only self, but enable those whom are also searching, traveling, to do so in a less encumbered way.

Each soul is likened unto a voyager upon a great sea of time and space and consciousness.

September 28

Will you see [your pet] again? To be sure. As you have the consciousness to perceive, then so will same occur and, perhaps you, in the next night, out of the corner of one eye might see a form and turn to see nothing but know, inwardly, of a friend's presence.

And, if there is permitted the opportunity to re-enter and to join again, not unlike the incarnative cycle of souls themselves, so, indeed, would [your pet] take on a new life, a new form, and the journey shall continue.

The direction of the intent, the work, the life's activities, the manner and such, of these creatures, is to a great degree under the dominion of their master or humankind in general. And so, it could be summarized succinctly here in the statement that, so as you give forth, is it returned to you many, many-fold over. And, once you have opened yourself and have given, it shall never end in returning to you from them.

Will you see [your pet] again? To be sure.

September 29

It is the right of each soul to seek its own need and its own purpose. If you allow another entity to claim that right, then, you have given the most precious gift idly away. Call that right back unto self. Identify your goal, your purpose, and record it, lest it not be lost in the influence or intentions of the daily activity. Hold that intent ever before you in times of challenge and/or opportunity, and know that, so as you do, all those forces which are His shall be with thee in your right to so do. See?

Identify your goal, your purpose, and record it, lest it not be lost in the influence or intentions of the daily activity.

September 30

Whenever there is a challenge or that which seems to be beyond what would be considered the blessings of God or a loving universe, it is wise to step back and to look with the eyes of wisdom and faith. For, as one does, there can be seen many forces of benevolent intent at work.

There are those who come upon challenge and do not meet it, neither do they accept that which is offered and, then, the journey becomes one of little or no accomplishment. The spirits then come forth to lift these up, that there can be a renewal and that there can be the brightness and hopefulness of their true being. That, as such, this might shine forth and show the way, and guide them into the claiming of their own beautiful uniqueness.

Whenever there is a challenge, there can be seen many forces of benevolent intent at work.

October 1

If ten entities gather together who have attained significant achievement in their life by following a certain path, and these ten, then, go into ten separate meeting rooms and invite you, collectively, to enter into each one, successively, whereupon each one tells you of their success by following a certain regimen, you could learn of the method that entity followed to attain their success, and you would have benefitted from it. But you may or may not have attained the same success, the same joy and happiness, as that entity. Then, does this mean that that entity's teaching is right or wrong, or does it mean that you should go on to the second?

Then, having completed the circuit of the entire ten, expending many Earth years so doing, all of the ten teachers come together in a great meeting with all of the students. The ten nod in unison and one of them stands, the spokesperson, and states, "All that we have given you is intended for perspective. You must find your own way," and they all depart. What then, dear friends? Frustration? Humor? Good cheer? Perhaps all of these. But one thing that will gradually evolve will be understanding that what was stated to you by the spokesperson was a truth.

Your pathway is as unique unto you as you are unto God. There is much to be gained by studying and learning of the achievements of those whom have made them. But all of this then must come back into self and arrive at that state of uniquely organized balance, which is you.

———

You must find your own way.

October 2

If you are excessive in your spiritual searching, the mind will likely be active right behind it, but, very often, the physical is left unto what remains … often, very little. There are many variations between the spiritual, the mental, the emotional, the physical, which could be reiterated here, but we believe that you all know that of what we speak.

Do keep a balance, physically, mentally, emotionally, spiritually, as often as you can, if not each and every Earth day. Don't let too many days pass by of intense activity at one of these levels of expression without countering them with some balancing activities on the others.

You can ignore these comments and suggestions and possibly show no visible effect from having so done for a goodly number of Earth years, or you may show no impact from having so done at all on the physical level. But, we assure you, there is an impact on these other levels, and you must meet it. In order to progress, you must learn to keep harmony, to keep balance.

Do keep a balance, physically, mentally, emotionally, spiritually, as often as you can, if not every Earth day.

October 3

This is a quest to discover the holiness that is thine ... as an ideal, yes, as a goal, as a purpose, also yes. But it is a quest to discover the holiness that is eternally you, and to bring this forth (so as thou art willing) as an offering unto others who would choose.

This is a quest to discover the holiness that is thine, and to bring this forth as an offering unto others who would choose.

October 4

You know not the power that is latent within you. Yet, you know the Promise and you know the hope that has been expressed for your future.

Even so, then, as the man called Jesus did His works and did them profoundly and frequently, these things can ye do, and more. You believe you cannot and, therefore, you cannot. But, when you believe you can, you will do them.

In a moment of belief, each of you have seen miracles. When that moment of belief grows to a minute or several minutes or, perhaps, even prolonged periods of time or days, then, you will do many miracles.

You know not the power that is latent within you.

October 5

As ye purify self to serve another, then, ye call upon that energy which is perfect and it will pass through thee as ye direct it and unto those works which thee then seek to do with it.

Comes the promise, the hope, the new testament.

Comes the promise, the hope, the new testament.

October 6

Where would one commence with showing mercy? Self. Have thee, dear friend, been merciful this day to self? Hast thou chastised self without good cause or reason? Have you burdened your mind, your spirit, with some attitude, with some punishment, with some perceived flaw or fault? Have you, by comparative judgment of self to others or to mass thought or habit, made for yourself an attitude which is less than joyful for this day?

Blessed are the merciful. Be merciful. Be understanding and compassionate with self that, by so doing, you can give this to others.

Blessed are the merciful. Be merciful. Be understanding and compassionate with self, that you can give this to others.

October 7

If self reaches that moment wherein the ego, the fears, the doubts, the limitations of that existence, can be placed aside for an instant (or through the training or the dedication, such can be made to occur quickly and easily), in either instance, this consciousness within self as an entity rises to the fore and guides with confidence and authority.

The actions which are guided through this inner knowing, this inner consciousness, are those which would lead thee to the Word, to the presence of God. Once this pathway is opened, then, His Word can flow through thee, just as surely as one who might create a channel for a body of water will find that the water will continue to affect the breadth and depth of its new channel.

The actions guided through inner knowing will lead thee to the Word, whereupon His Word can flow through thee.

October 8

You may think in the collective sense that mind is a tool of consciousness when consciousness chooses to manifest itself into the finite. Mind is that tool which is used by consciousness to create. Mind is that which seeks to know itself in finiteness and, as such, then, becomes cognizant of itself in Consciousness (capital C). Mind is that quality of spirit which has an intent to be manifest and to understand its manifestation and, thus, to comprehend the nature of the dimensions or variations of finiteness. Mind is that which can see and do according to the will.

The will is moreso associated to spirit.

Spirit is intended to have dominion over the mind. Mind in the Earth often does not accept this but, rather, is subjugated by the force of "mass-mind" thought ... the collective nature of those forces or energies which either are used or unused and, thus, the power associates with that which is the strongest or most dominant.

Consciousness knows, and knowing does not require thinking, contemplation, in the sense of evaluating, adjudicating, and all that sort. When you are Consciousness in the Earth, you are the Christ, in a manner of speaking. See?

If you perceive from finiteness, it is understandable that you could consider that all that is or ever shall be is already in existence, for, finiteness has, by the matter of its own definition, definition. Consciousness is unlimited, ever expanding, alive, as God is alive, making all existence possible.

Mind acts according to the will. Consciousness knows, and knowing does not require thinking, contemplation.

October 9

The path of righteousness awaits those in the Earth consciousness who are willing to free themselves enough to move unto it. It is not something you accomplish through intensity of effort, but through the ease of joy held in you in all things, through your recognition that there is naught that can endure greater than thee ... that, whatsoever there is that might be taken from thee, the measure of that that will be given in return can not be estimated in its beauty and its grandeur and in its sweetness.

Your world, the world which is called the Earth and so much more than this ... which embraces unseen expressions of what is called the Earth, are poised on the threshold of purification. What you choose, thereafter ... Believe it, build it, share it. But, most of all, free yourselves.

As has been given here, and elsewhere to be sure, again and again: Whatsoever you can do with the grace of God to free all that is within you and lift it up, that it can be born again anew, this, then, you do unto all. This, then, becomes the gift that you have to give.

Whatever you can do to free all that is within you and lift it up, this you do unto all and it becomes the gift you give.

October 10

There are many souls in and about the Earth who are enduring challenge during these current times. Thus, it is good and of a kind heart that you would pause often to remember them, that you can provide a pathway unto them according to God's Holy Law that can be traversed to bring to them ease and healing and a sense of peace in the face of challenge.

It is good and of a kind heart that you would pause often to remember the many souls enduring challenge in these times.

October 11

There are those who committed heinous acts in the past who are living lives that are a symbol of the Light in the present. And the opposite is true ... that there are those who were angelic-like in their past lives are now experiencing the darkness of misdeeds in the Earth.

So, good not to judge in the sense that one knoweth not all of the ramifications of this.

Good not to judge in the sense that one knoweth not all of the ramifications of this.

October 12

No, the Hall of Records has not been opened. There has been a growing energy around these and, in the etheric, there is the approach of greater balance and light, and some additional activity in the area of the guardians of this knowledge. It is possible that this will occur within the next decade, but we do not see it at present as opened. You will know this by the effect it has, do you see.

We can only state here, dear friend, that this is possible within your lifetime. Whether or not it is to be is in the hearts and minds, moreso than the hands, of thy brothers and sisters who are dwelling in the Earth realm. Unless there is that state of harmony and peace that can make the way open and passable for the Teacher of Righteousness to come forth, then, it shall not open. Understand that it is of a nature that could be misused with considerable ease and it would be a misadventure to be given to those who had not reached that state of peaceful joy, the righteousness that is the Father's. See?

The Hall of Records has not been opened. You will know this by the effect it has, do you see.

October 13

There is no offering here that can temper the loss of a loved one in the Earth. For, surely, as one gathers the light of joy and happiness from friendship or family or child about them, and that light moves from their presence, would there not be a sense of loss?

But the recognition needs to be focused and emphasized upon the fact that that light does not go out nor diminish, but becomes more brilliant as it passes through that veil of separateness between your realm and these. The love, which is a part of being together in the Earth, does not cease. It expands and multiplies.

Those moments which are together, ye and those whom are loved ... Let them be meaningful, and let each moment be as precious as the bird which might fly from the branch in the next moment. See?

Let each moment be as precious as the bird which might fly from the branch in the next moment.

October 14

One of the greatest expressions of true love is being or having a true friend.

If each entity entering into a matrimonial relationship sought, first, vigorously to develop an attitude of true friendship between their potential mate and self, all would stay together, or they wouldn't have the relationship in the first place ... They'd be such good friends, they'd recognize their differences were too great. See?

One of the greatest expressions of true love is being or having a true friend.

October 15

Limitation is an illusion, but it is real when it is sub-scribed to. And the reality becomes greater just so as the number of believers or subscribers becomes greater, until such time that the illusion seems to be greater than the Promise.

It shall be our continual prayer for your ascension above that illusion, and that the kingdom of our Father within you and that which is the eternal Kingdom here become as one.

Limitation is an illusion, but it is real when subscribed to.

October 16

"What is a dream, truly?" the Master asks. "That which one believes, or that which one thinks is only illusion? And how does one differentiate?

"Is slumber the doorway through which one passes from reality into illusion? Or could it be possible," and the Master laughs softly, "that the reverse is true ... that the illusion is here," tapping on the rail that He is perched on, "and that truth and reality lie beyond," tapping His forefinger on His heart, "here. That we enter this, the Kingdom of God and the truth of God, through the portal called sleep."

Is slumber the doorway through which one passes from reality into illusion, or could it be that the reverse is true?

October 17

Some walk upon the Earth with the light of their oneness with God emanating from them. That light, in the manner of their life's choice, the path they have walked upon, and their words, their actions ... All of this, bears the essence of that light. Many of these, the faithful, choose pathways which are according to what they feel, that to which they are drawn as an affinity or a resonance or a call. In the majesty and beauty of these souls and their works, in the presence of the Master, the Christ, we tell you many of these have stopped short of what they could have been or could be.

This is not to minimize, but to proclaim: The greater glory is always ahead. It is to encourage you to let their examples be shining lights, which you can move into and out of in times of need, for respite, for replenishing, rebalancing.

Believe unto self, as He has given it. Believe that you can. Believe that it is possible. Be willing to release that which tells you it is not so.

In the questions of one's heart or mind, when dealing with challenges in the Earth, there can be found answers aplenty. When you see these and nod and state, "Yes, but ..." perhaps, that will be the inspiration that you need to not stop short with your faith. When you believe that you have reached a point of utter faithfulness, take another step and another, and go beyond it. See?

When you believe that you have reached a point of utter faithfulness, take another step and another, and go beyond it.

October 18

The pathway of "sacrifice" and the purging of all worldly goods and interests might be thought of as "passive." For a term which can be applied to the opposite, we would choose "the active principle." The passive becomes opened to discern guidance from beyond the Earth to impact, to a degree, the effectiveness of the higher consciousness to mass-mind thought, gradually permeating same and changing the nature of it, that the entirety of the souls therein involved might find their peace, might find their willful acceptance of their higher nature.

The active, which is often most favoritely associated with the Christ, is to engage in the Earth full-on, participating in activities preponderant in that historical time frame, and demonstrates that, in spite of these "constraints" (from the passive perspective), one can apply right thinking, right living, and the basic tenets, and accomplish the same, if not more expediently, with more dramatic results than the passive.

Perhaps surprisingly to many., you can actually embrace both … Purge yourself of those bonds which confine your heart, your emotion, your thinking, to the Earth; and, in the outer as relates to your actions and words and deeds, become the example and, the moreso the passive takes effect within you, you can become a worker of the highest light and the most profound accomplishment. You can walk in both worlds. It does not divide you. It maximizes the highest aspects of both, for the highest possible service to God and to mankind.

You can actually embrace both, active and passive principles,
Maximizing the best aspects for the hishest possible service.

October 19

Focus on yourself, and have others focus on you, too, for, within this body is a soul of great beauty ... one of strength, determination, spontaneity, joy, and effervescence.

Conversely, we have all of these qualities in hiding within this body. Won't you bring them forth? Others can't do this. They may try. They may alter the result of that for a time. They may give you strength to change some habits, some ways of living, some mechanisms, but, until you use the potential within your being, no permanent change can be anticipated.

Until you use the potential within your being, no permanent change can be anticipated.

October 20

If you begin from the within and work towards the outer,
you can accomplish anything.

If you begin on the outer and expect the inner to change,
this is as casting words into the wind ... Someone might hear
them downwind, but those who are upwind surely won't.

Thy spirit holds the key, the power, and the potential.

If you begin from the within and work towards the outer, you
can accomplish anything.

October 21

There are those forces now very much in motion. There is the expectation that, after the occurrence of many of these events, there shall be the realignment of mankind, humanity, towards a more common goal. That, thereafter, there would come the focus upon the needs and wants of all peoples according to a universal pattern or scheme, rather than the isolationist pocket of consciousness and belief.

This force which is in motion, of course, that which is categorically called "Earth changes" and these are fast upon the Earth. The effects of this can be seen, as given previously: First, in the climate ... the changes, the pattern, the shifts. Secondly, in the hearts and minds of humankind. Thirdly, in the Earth itself.

But, if you would, consider that significant Earth changes would predicate a shift in focus of what is important, what is of value, and the need for some degree of cooperation and alignment of entities, each to the other, in mutual service for the betterment of all.

Therefore, all aspects of Earth changes as an aftermath or aftereffect are seen to be, at the minimum, productive.

Significant Earth changes predicate a shift in focus of what is important, of value, and the need for mutual service for all.

October 22

In recent times, some of you have lost entities in the physical sense from your lives ... some of you through movement of loved ones through the veil of separateness between the Earth realm and beyond, others of you through circumstances and events which have caused you to feel without love or, perhaps more accurately, without a channel through which you might give your love in the manner you had either hoped for or become accustomed to.

We ask you in humbleness to consider ... In the days ahead, open yourself and find out how your love will always be fulfilled, how you can be in the Earth and know complete love, how you can always feel and know that your love has a place to be given and that, in so choosing, so shall you receive as you give.

Life, the grand illusion, for, it seems so permanent, so challenging and, so often, all that is.

Learn that you are greater than this, and learn that love can never be destroyed. It is like your own being, your own spirit. It can only be transformed.

Remember now many of The Master's Teachings about Love: Love can set you free. Love is the power that heals. Love is the power that surmounts all and challenges nothing. Love exists as a small particle or a great mountain within all.

Perhaps, you can begin the process of following His guidance. Pray on this. Meditate on it, and set yourselves free.

Love can never be destroyed. It is like your own being, your own spirit ... It can only be transformed.

October 23

Friendship. Jesus loved the disciples. He became friends with them and they with He. He offered them all that He had. He withheld naught, but offered openly.

The disciples could often be seen radiating some form of light. Some thought, because they were close physically to the Master here or there, that He had placed this light around them, but He had not placed an orb of light around them in that sense. He had connected with them eternally. He knew, prior to His entry, who they were, where they were, and when to call them. It was merely the act, therefore, of making the connection. First, physically, then, mentally. Then, most lastingly, spiritually ... a line of loving light so that, if a single disciple was a great distance away from the Master or was at works after the Master had returned to the kingdom of our Father, that connection of light remained. As that disciple, sought to claim that connection, that offering of friendship, they could let their hands be as the Master's hands to become the instruments of healing works.

You have aligned yourselves with the same Source of love. Therefore, as did the disciples, you can also do. You are empowered, not impotent.

As did the disciples, you can also do. You are empowered, not impotent.

October 24

You are majestic in the capacity to answer a need because the majesty of God is the light, the love, centered within you.

But, it is similar to your electric light bulb … It doesn't shed much illumination until it's turned on, until the switch is thrown to cause the electrical flow and such to energize it.

You are like a light bulb connected by a line of light to God. You are the only one who has control of the switch. Try it. Turn it on. Let a little light of love shine forth today.

You are majestic in the capacity to answer a need because the majesty of God is the light, the love, centered within you.

October 25

We come in service as followers to the Master, the Christ.
There are none who are in the Earth and who have been
in the Earth who speak of goodness and brotherhood and the
qualities that are of the Father's goodness – none – that we
do not claim as our brother and sister.

We see many in the Earth who follow pathways that seem
divergent. As you hear the words and the prayers and the
methods and all that sort, we humbly encourage you to set
this aside if it appears divergent from your belief, and feel the
spirit of their faith and honor this, whether their actions are
in agreement with what you hold to be righteous or nay.

We are all one. Cast aside the illusion, and set yourself
free. As you do this, this one simple act, you will have given a
blessing to the Mother-Earth and to your brethren.

Set this aside if it appears divergent from your belief, and feel
the spirit of their faith and honor this.

October 26

The power is in the prayer and in the belief in what is said and done.

Do not believe yourselves to be weak or helpless. Know yourself to be the Father's eternal Child. He, within you, doeth the work as you seek and ask and offer it.

The power is in the prayer and in the belief in what is said and done.

October 27

The capacity to raise thy thought to a point wherein, in a moment, in an instant, thou art aware of thy perfect nature, and the knowledge of this plus the knowledge of earthly activities imparted the aspect of forgiveness and grace as a giant spiritual eraser might erase misconceptions, judgments, guilts … So was He aware of this capacity and, thus, used this in God's name.

One has but to think and to believe to have it done.

One has but to think and to believe to have it done.

October 28

Blessed are the peacemakers for they shall be called or known as the children of God.

You understand, of course, dear friends, what it means to be a child, and you know within yourselves that you all are children of God. So, what can this mean, to be recognized as a child of God ... to be titled, child of God?

It is clearly that you, yourself, would claim your Heritage.

If you strive for peace within yourself you enable the claiming of your Heritage.

If you strive for peace within yourself you enable the claiming of your own Heritage.

October 29

The truth within you is likened unto a temple of light.

All things can be seen, if thou would take whatsoever is your quest, your need, into this temple of truth within you. Therein, it shall be seen according to the will of God and according to that which is never by the interpretation of one or more outwardly, for, theirs is conditioned by that which they hold as their quest, as their need, or as that which had brought them to their current point of being.

But, the temple of truth within you shines clearly, with honor and truth for all things.

The temple of truth within you shines clearly, with honor and truth for all things.

October 30

We would consider abundance as being that nature of existence which acknowledges and accepts the unlimited nature and flow of abundance from God. In other words, abundance is the mechanism, the way of living. Prosperity, then, would be defined moreso as the result of that way of living, the manifestation of the entity's choice that is likened unto the fruit of an effort.

So, it could be stated that, when one lives a life cognizant of the abundant nature of God and claims same as their own heritage, their life becomes evidentially prosperous, whether or not that prosperity is defined in terms of the purely materialistic or some variation of that. In other words, it is important for you to understand, yourself, what your definition and goal might be in regard to the fruit of living an abundant life.

When one lives cognizant of the abundant nature of God and claims same as their heritage, their life becomes prosperous.

October 31

What is prayer? Well, perhaps it is so that you are praying to an entity who is seated upon a glorious throne some many billions of light years away, at the edge of your universe and that that entity is, in fact, God. And that 'round and about His glorious throne can be seen legions of angels and holy servants whose wills are completely submitted unto His.

Or, it could be so that the God unto who you issue your prayer lives within the same body as do you … breathing the same air, eating the same foods, and experiencing exactly what you experience, step by step, moment by moment, traveling with you through this lifetime.

It is, perhaps, obvious to you that we would, of course, opt for the latter definition moreso than the former.

These words are given to you in the spirit of oneness with God, in the essence of that within you which knows its way Home: That which you are praying to is within you. Therefore, the power to answer the prayer must also be therein.

You are the power which can answer the prayer that you issue. It is through you and of you that the prayer will be answered. Even if that is difficult for you to accept, even if you cannot find yourself, in any sense of the word, worthy of such power, nonetheless, it is yours.

You are the power which can answer the prayer that you issue, through you and of you.

November 1

No one becomes a master without acquiring grace, for they are synonymous. The grace of God is the Word of God. So as God speaks to man, so does man apply these words, these guidances, to gain grace. Thus, the man Jesus gained grace by His experiences collectively to that point, and the Christ and the man Jesus united through God's grace. It is as to say that a child returned to the father by the experiences which were fostered. See?

Grace is the ability for one to learn from their experiences. Grace is also the opportunity to avoid self-judgment as a result of a finite point of view. Grace is the expression of God's love actively participating in your lives, in your experiences. See?

Grace is the expression of God's love actively participating in your lives, in your experiences.

November 2

You are living in what we shall call the yang experience. Yet, all that you are, all that you do, has its reaction and its shared result in the yin. There is a veil, delicate in nature, transparent in its essence of mobility through itself, that separates.

As the Light comes into the Earth, it comes into the yin, as well and, then, there must be the sharing of this. For, the yielding/the submissive/the passive, and the outgoing/the moreso aggressive ... These are like particles orbiting around a nuclei which, in and of their own nature, possess the full potential of creative power. It becomes a question of how one is willing to understand and perceive themselves and their own position in the universal forces. If you prefer to think in terms of polarities defined by male and female bodies and, if you wish to think of that as man and woman, that is your right and your choice. If, as we pray, you shall think from time to time of yourself as unlimited, then, the entirety of our Father's kingdoms are at your command.

Each of you possesses the beauty and the strength of both yin and yang. Each of you has the pathway unto the mysteries and the source of all nourishment, and, as well, unto that which is the Light of lights, the Spark of existence. It remains only for you to recognize and, then, to use these, that ye shall become, *made manifest in Earth*, Children of God.

Each of you possesses the beauty and the strength of both yin and yang.

November 3

In your thoughts, in your attitudes, those things which thou thinketh and believe and hold in your heart, they are you. Spirit is the pattern, mind is the builder, and the physical is the result. This has been given through Edgar oft times and elsewhere, to be sure. Let's expand on that just a bit … Not only is the physical the result but, through habit, if not fondness with a certain way of thinking and acting, so do you become this in your mental body, in your emotional being, and body. And while your spirit is ever, at its highest level of expression, one with God, this aspect of your being is limited by the attitude, the thought.

What you believe, what thou thinketh in thine heart, so art thou. It is inescapable. It can be masked. It can be obscured from the vision, for the greater part at least, from others in the Earth. An entity can go through their life seemingly, to the general public, one thing and, inwardly, be something else. These are usually seen in the spiritual body or energy field of an entity in the Earth. They are felt by those of you who feel these things while you are in the Earth. In these realms, we see this as the "spiritual cloak," as we call it, which is not the physical form but the essence of the entity. The cloak, then, is distorted by these thought-forms, these thought essences.

Through habit, fondness with a way of thinking and acting, so do you become this in your mental and emotional being.

November 4

Breathe in, ever, the peace of God. Breathe it in until you live it, until it becomes who you are.

Know the love of God. Know it to be without limit. Know the honor of oneness with God to be beyond limitation.

Hold the truth of God within you, for, this is the spirit of the Father, giving life to all that is.

Meet that which comes unto thee with compassion, and allow it to pass through you unchanged as it wishes; but, whenever such turns to ask of you, give unto it that eternal blessing of the Father that gives life to all: His grace. May the peace of God go before you in all that you are.

Be free.

Breathe in, ever, the peace of God. Breathe it in until you live it, until it becomes who you are.

November 5

There is naught in the Earth that God has not already forgiven. Do what you must to open your heart and to feel free of guilt and sin and, certainly, take action to enable you to affirm that you are free of this while you are yet in the Earth.

And if you cannot do this, remember these words when you do pass through the veil of separateness between the Earth and the beyond. That, in a time thereafter, should you be limited, you might remember to open and receive the prayers, which we and others like us and many in the Earth who are growing in number, offer prayer constantly, to help free those who are limited, those who are in, as called, the Sea of Faces.

Open your heart to feel free of guilt and sin, that you are free of this while you are yet in the Earth.

November 6

It is the intent and spirit with which thou doeth all things, whether they be great or small, that brings to thy path the greater light. It is, truly, upon the arms that thou hast helped that ye shall be led into the kingdoms of our Father. It shall be through the rejoicing and light of those who have been recipients of your loving prayer whose joy and light shall greet thee as you pass through the veil. It is the small act of kindness that shall endow you with a cloak of light when you leave behind the cloak of flesh and finiteness of the Earth.

Measure yourself and your life according to the ideal within. And, ever, look to this ideal to see, Is it truly the highest and best that I can perceive? And are the steps along the way, the goals, and the purposes by which I do what I do, in the image of that ideal?"

Lastly, we would offer to you these simple truths: There is one unto whom we ask you in humbleness to give your love without limitation. There is one in the Earth we would ask you to forgive without any reservation. There is one whom we would encourage you to support and nurture and to do all good things unto. And that is self. For, it is that same self which is the vessel unto which shall bear all other things to those whom you shall meet in life. Within you is the cup which can and does hold the very spirit of God, that which is present to fulfill the spiritual need or thirst of others.

Within you is the cup which holds the very spirit of God, present to fulfill the spiritual need or thirst of others.

November 7

A lamp has its light within and. as such, casts it all around. It would be well if you would do likewise. For, if you honor self, then, you have honored God, and you will surely, thereafter, honor others. See?

If you honor self, then, you have honored God, and you will surely, thereafter, honor others.

November 8

The mind is like an immense tablet upon which is inscribed all experiences ... the thoughts, the emotions, all that
has gone before throughout all of consciousness. And, yet, as
great as all that could be recorded upon this tablet might be,
a vast area upon it remains waiting to be inscribed.

If you were to inscribe upon your tablet that which you
would have come to pass, how would it read?

If you were to inscribe upon your tablet that which you
would have come to pass, how would it read?

November 9

Some entities issue yo-yo prayers. That sort of prayer goes out and then is drawn back, and goes out and then is drawn back. Faith is the down-swing, where the prayer goes out. And doubt calls it back. Be a bit cautious not to issue yo-yo prayers.

Be a bit cautious not to issue yo-yo prayers.

November 10

The greater soul, the God-consciousness of self, knows this current time in the Earth to be one of particularly powerful acceleration and, in that wisdom of knowledge, recognizes that the potential here is very significant, although rather delicately balanced for most. The power of the current incarnation, in terms of what can be accomplished, should not be underestimated. The potential at the soul level is great.

Thou art in the Earth in the present. Look for the joy and look for the purposeful works which shall invoke the greater qualities of your soul and the fulfillment of a joyous existence. How might you do this? Be thankful for the commencement of each new day, considering it a blessing from God.

These are those times which have been foretold, where those who seek and strive shall be known and claimed by the forces of God. Thus, look into the heart of self and find that which, by its nature, might bring thee joy, and to seek it.

Look for the joy and look for the purposeful works which shall invoke the greater qualities of your soul.

November 11

The feet need more care. Manipulation, massage to these, soaking them often, will do nearly as much to stabilizing your body and your glandular secretions as any other single action. All too often, entities ignore the important function the feet play in spiritual evolvement. Be mindful that the Master and those about Him knew this. He taught them. The most spiritual and blessed gift they could give was to cleanse one another's feet, to manipulate them, and to bring them into a state of harmony, ease, and balance, by so doing.

It is a practice which would do well to be revived as a symbol of spiritual love and as a gift to one another. In this, a reflexologist would assist much of this for you. Soaking them is also very important.

The feet need more care. All too often, entities ignore the important function the feet play in spiritual evolvement.

November 12

Words from this collective source would fall vastly short of describing, in terms of comprehension in your minds, the meaning of "God is Love" ...

The capacity of each soul to create, in the micro/macrocosmic sense, all that they desire, regardless of the effect and influence upon any other forces. Be they subjective, be they those which are collective, or those which are random, by definition, the ability to allow growth on the basis of individual wishes.

God is the capacity – expressed in the term "love" – to be silent. See?

God is the capacity – expressed in the term "love" – to be silent.

November 13

The interpretations of your statement "God has never, will never, and can never express anything but love" that would seem to fault this statement are just that ... interpretations from a finite point of view. When one finds some experience which they would think would disprove this statement, then, that is the time for you to begin your works. For, to understand that each entity is unrestricted in their ability to create is to understand that love must be present to permit this to occur. For example, in an ordered structure, things need to conform in order to be in harmony with law. Law is thought to be a restricting, guiding, though often valuable, course of thought. But God's Law is that each soul is completely independent, is completely without restriction, limitation, or reservation. So, His Law is to preserve the total freedom of your consciousness.

God is. God is love, compassion, assistance, harmony. God is, and the aspect of love is one of the highest manifestations of the presence of God. When one expresses love – not physical love, not a sexual act, not physical contact, not the attitude of one towards another, but, love in the sense of complete joy, an expressed fulfilling love for life, for consciousness, for existence, and for its opportunities – then one begins to realize God. See?

When one expresses love, an expressed fulfilling love for life, for consciousness, then one begins to realize God.

November 14

All things are of God. The force as called "demonic" relates to polarity and to activities which are relegated by a defining and delineating point of view as negative. There are, in effect, forces which are detrimental or negative or "evil" to your intent. These are the collective thoughts and attitudes, which exist in a realm which have been agreed upon to function within said thoughts and attitudes.

All things are of God. The creation of an evil force is the result of the thoughts and attitudes of individual souls or entities traversing their own experiences. These forces have no greater or lesser effect upon any soul than that entity expressed through that soul is willing to accept.

The creation of an evil force is the result of the thoughts and attitudes of individual souls traversing their own experiences.

November 15

The greatest "sin" in the Earth plane is merely an opportunity for one or more entities to experience. If, by that experience, they learn the greater value of the meaning of eternal love, or grace, or compassion, then, how can one state that the experience is evil, if the result is of such beauty?

The greatest "sin" in the Earth plane is merely an opportunity for one or more entities to experience.

November 16

Man is the expression of spirit, finite in a finite existence which has been collectively agreed upon by souls.

It is quite this simple ... that, so as you believe, is it.

The teachings through Matthew are exceptionally clear, in that they denote the responsibility of each entity to recognize of their own free will, their own volition, their participation and oneness with a far greater environ than that which is defined in the finite sense.

Your world is, in essence, an illusion. It is that which exists by mutual consent, by mutual understanding, and by mutual acceptance. If thee would go beyond this and accept the infinite nature of your being, you would recognize that, as long as you desired to function within those premises, you can expand infinitely upon that which has been agreed upon and you can help and guide unto the purpose of the mass and in accord with, and in service to, the Christ.

Man is the expression of spirit, finite in a finite existence which has been agreed upon by souls, collectively.

November 17

When you are in the sleep state, the spiritual is vibrant, alive with light and curiosity, interested in works to be done, for, anything that has been a part of your event or happenstance during the just previous Earth day is worked upon in the sleep state. Records are retrieved, karma is reviewed, opportunities are looked at, plans are made and discussed, and many entities are met and an exchange of consciousness takes place again and again. And there are those times which are simply for the renewal of your spirit, your mind, your heart, that you shall awaken carrying that renewal into your physical body and the events following in the day which shall resume upon your awakening.

You may meet and interact with other entities of like spiritual light. You may sing, you may dance, you may dwell in the light or you may rest. You may study, you may go on holiday, you may take time to have good laughter with those whom you revere. You may join those whom have left the Earth before you and you may join those who have not yet entered, or you may help a soul who is in need by going to them in your spiritual essence while your body sleeps. You may come together as a group and do group works. You may strive to heal thought-forms and consciousness. You may journey to other realms and seek knowledge or wisdom or do a work of grace in our Father's name.

When you are in the sleep state, the spiritual is vibrant, alive with light and curiosity, interested in works to be done.

November 18

To teach one's own consciousness a lack of limitation is, in essence, to destroy their references to the physical plane. To teach one another the unlimited nature of their beings is to gain the blessings of the physical plane. The difference being that, united or collective, you provide strength and you compose a basic theorem or set of laws.

So it was that souls agreed upon points of reference for progression. By intensely focusing their consciousness, there was the awareness of the Earth. By concurring to certain premises, souls entered and became in harmony by expression. They also learned disharmony by expression ... the variations of thoughts, attitudes, emotions and deeds are all aspects of learning harmony.

So, in studying love, in studying how to manifest love, you must know and understand and be willing to accept the expressions of discord or lack of harmony in others because you know that, ultimately, they will arrive at a point of awareness which will show them how to construct all of these experiences into a harmonious state. Because you remember them from a time wherein you agreed, all of you, to enter the Earth plane because these experiences would be of value, you also know within your being that you are all a part of a vast, harmonious existence.

In studying how to manifest love, you must understand, be willing to accept, the expressions of discord or lack in others.

November 19

It is this change that brings to the Earth one of the greatest opportunities it has seen in two thousand Earth years. Should we, then, join the others in foreboding doom or apocalyptic catastrophe?

We cannot serve that which is outside of what we find here, nor alter it to be in harmony with that of a group or a mass. Were we to do so, that would conclude these works. So, we can give only that which we find before us as we find it. As we attempt to give it to you, in terms or phrases which are, as we perceive them, best intended for your understanding on all levels, not just one, there can be the appearance here and there of something which is not present in the words, the statements ... but, rather, is present where? In your thoughts? In the thoughts and words of others?

Listen very carefully to what we give next, for it is given openly and without precursive intent, but to bear Truth: You are the hope of the future. You have in your heart a spark, the will to seek beyond the known and accepted, and to reach beyond the veil, whether deemed illusionary or real, to know truth at its deepest and most profound level.

You are the hope of the future.

November 20

Take a moment, and consider this ...

We have all journeyed through many lifetimes, in many different ways. We have tasted the fruit of each vine of the Earth, the fruit of each tree. We have held in our hands the creations of all the arrays in existence. We have smelled and touched and tasted all that there is to do and, now, we have lifted up into a state of heavenly bliss, Nirvana. Here we are. We are one.

You look around in Nirvana and see many beautiful, beautiful beings of Light.

But you will find that most here, after a time, choose to go somewhere else, and the reason for that is that they find joy in giving. They find that the continuation of this bliss, this wonderful time of absolute bliss is delicious and, so, can you conceive of such a thing? Reaching Nirvana and choosing to leave it?

While you're considering that, contemplate the possibility that it is you of whom we speak.

Can you conceive of such a thing? Reaching Nirvana and choosing to leave it?

November 21

When you celebrate the transition of a loved one, you celebrate for them, but there is, no less, the sense of loss. For, the Earth or any such is compromised of substance, and that substance is experienced, known, felt, tasted, smelled, heard, seen, and it becomes the definition of your reality. The greater there is that attachment to any aspect or aspects of same, then, the moreso the removal of that aspect does leave (what you would colloquially call) a hole, a vacuum.

But, if you have, in the journey prior, builded that which can be called upon to fill that void – to fill it with the love and laughter, with the light of the sight that has been gained and shared – there is the realization that here is a cause for celebration. A tear or two, yes. For, something is, in fact, gone, but it is, you see, never lost.

The choices are many, and you can choose, just as they; but, if you have builded that moment in the journey where you paused to look into the heart of one another, remember what you saw therein ... It remains.

See?

Where you paused to look into the heart of one another, remember what you saw. It remains.

November 22

Miracles are the ability of an entity to overcome the expected need or result by applying the Law of Truth and the Law of Grace, utilized through their own free will and given fuel or energy from an expression of love freely given ... no matter what the circumstance, no matter what the environ. Miracles occur out of grace. An entity who has achieved a state of grace becomes, thereafter, a teacher of righteousness, for, their life becomes the living expression of the Laws of God: They are balanced in their Free Will and their choice of living in an expression of Love, and they open the portal for Truth to be the demonstrated pattern of their work, their will. So doing, they open a channel of blessings by which the Law of Grace can make itself manifest, through which miracles are performed which seem to be capable of transgressing all other laws. The Law of Grace is the key, the ultimate tool with which all things can be met, all things can be accomplished.

Many miracles have been done, and many more await being done. Those which have been completed need only to be claimed, and the reality shall be made firm in the Earth. Those which yet remain to be done are unopened gifts now being held out before you in the outstretched hands of God. If it be thy will to claim them then, thereof, ye shall find an everlasting joy and oneness.

Miracles are the ability to overcome a need or result by applying the Laws of Truth and Grace, through Free Will and Love.

November 23

What is desire? Desire is, ultimately, a memory. It is the intuitive, eternal knowledge within self that there is a perfect way of existence, unlimited, and filled with a joy and radiance incomparable in any other finite expression. No matter what the stimuli might be externally in the Earth to cause you to have desire, there shall always be a seed from the ocean of God's Spirit at the core of that which motivates you.

As you move through the process of desiring something, you evaluate your progress by action and reaction, which can be sensory, internal (as in emotion), or intuitive (as in the spiritual memory) and it will, ultimately, be all of those. These become your feelings, your emotions. Knowing these things, you strive to be the master of them, so, you go within self to the very core of your being where the light of your own drop-let of God's Spirit still is, and you think, you contemplate, you become aware. Thought is that which works in harmony with the universal forces to build the pattern, the image, of the desire and emotion.

Yet, it is not about you in the Earth and, therefore, you must find that which compares most closely to it. You will always seek it. You are a drop of water from the ocean which is God. As you seek, remember that. You are always a part of the ocean, and the ocean a part of you. You have but only to affirm that and live your life as though it were true.

There shall always be a seed from the ocean of God's Spirit at the core of that which motivates you.

November 24

Man exists that he might know himself and, thus, know God and, thus, be at-one with God and, thus, co-create and coexist with God and, thus, be absorbed and absorb the love, the wonder, of God, and so on and so on.

Man exists as an image of his true being for experience and for enlightenment to be capable of accepting his own infinite nature.

Man exists that he might know himself and, thus, know God.

November 25

Guides are those entities or, if you prefer, those souls, who have, more often than not, also experienced just so as you are experiencing in the Earth.

There may often be more than one guide. The interaction between these guides, who vary in their number with each of you in the Earth, is somewhat dependent upon the choices which were made prior to entry into the Earth. The primary guides, as they might be called, were present during those times of decision-making and they have, for the most part, been with you throughout the entirety of your sojourns to the current point and will continue to be present with you until the conclusion of your current incarnation, and will guide you to your rightful position of spiritual acceptance, thereafter.

The company of guides is also enhanced by many other beautiful souls, whose joyous participation and wisdom can be called upon in any moment of need. These can include entities from what you know of as many different realms of consciousness and/or expression, including the Elders who serve in oneness with the Master, the Christ.

Guides are those entities who have, more often than not, also experienced just so as you are experiencing in the Earth.

November 26

Don't think for a moment that you cannot ascend over any challenge in the Earth. Whether you use the power of prayer, God's Grace, or His Universal Law as your tools or mechanisms of accomplishment, these are matters of your choice. For, you are workers in our Father's Kingdom and He has not called you to do a work and given you no tools. In the contrary, He has given you great and numerous tools, so many that their number is beyond expression. For every single need, no matter how great or small, there are many tools from which you might choose.

In your very next Earth day, you will probably meet a challenge of limitation, slight or great. It is our prayer that you will remember some of these words, some of this information, and you will think of that as an opportunity of ascension of your own. That, as you meet and rise above any limitation, you have ascended one step closer to the kingdom of your own potential and oneness with God.

Don't think for a moment that you cannot ascend over any challenge in the Earth.

November 27

Clear your minds occasionally. Remove the clutter and those effects which are brought about through daily living in a society which, in a general sense, has forgotten its own voyage. From this, then, shall you build footings, a foundation. The cleansing of one's mind, or tidying up, if you prefer, cannot easily be done if one seeks to simply force what they consider errant thought from their mind. Rather, one should look at each thought, whether considered errant or nay, and determine with honor and respect to themselves from whence has this its origin.

If one thinks of a thought that, in review, seems hostile to thy brethren, a few moments' searching will find some source which is a point of service, a point of change, needed within thy being. To suppress this thought or simply keep it (as one might state humorously) at thy ears, this would not complete the needed experience. Rather, as one learns from those thoughts which are manifested, then comes the preparation, which is of beauty, of wonder.

Best mechanism for clearing away cluttered thoughts? Meditation, of course. Prayer, for some. Interaction with groups, as in those who pray together. And, service to others often cleanses and clears clutter from one's mind and, my, how this delights the spirit!

Service to others often cleanses and clears clutter from one's mind, and, my, how this delights the spirit and mind!

November 28

Some might ask the question, what is peace? Others might ask, and how do you differentiate peace from what you call the Peace of God?

We here would define peace as that state attained by one who journeys in definition or finiteness having attained a state of balance. Generally speaking, in definition, or incarnation, it is having attained those things expected of one, those things which are implied as necessities to reach a state of peaceful existence.

Contrasting that, the Peace of God is the state of being in which all is experienced as good or joyful. There are no requirements in the latter. There are no expectations. There is only its presence awaiting you, each of you, to reach out and partake of same.

The Peace of God is the state of being in which all is experienced as good or joyful.

November 29

What is the relationship between the mind and the spirit? Is the mind an eternal part of the spirit, or is the mind, as it is known in Earth, merely a byproduct of the spiritual self that is seeking to gain, or to contribute, or both in that journey?

The mind is the tool of the spirit that is intended to be as a steppingstone, that the eternal consciousness and wisdom of spirit can be brought to the level of expression in the definition called finiteness, and that the accomplishments in finiteness can, thus, be delivered to the spirit.

The mind is, then, a pathway, if you will, of expression or exchange between the potential and the manifest and from the manifest to the potential, that (in the case of the latter) the potential can grow and, through the growth of the potential, what is called the Universe, then, continues its expansion and acceleration.

It is the pulse of creation. It is the thrust of that intent that that which is given is received and, in the receipt, is multiplied and, in the multiplication, becomes manifest as consciousness, and that that consciousness, then, can know itself.

The mind is a pathway of expression or exchange between the potential and the manifest.

November 30

It is written that none knoweth the hour, the day, of our Master's return. Thus, we offer this, again, as given through Edgar: When those who are His have made the way passable, He shall return.

We can repeat that, if needed, for, it appears there is a lack of understanding or clarity. (If so, understand that we claim the credit for this, with a note of loving humor.) So, we have offered it again here, in humble love.

What you can do is be who you are ... the fire that is the breath of God, which lives eternally as you.

Be who you are ... the fire that is the breath of God, which lives eternally as you.

December 1

As we find it, Jesus and the Christ became one through that soul's development and acceptance directly from God. So, the Christ would be that spirit which is found in every entity and which is accepted or rejected to the greater or lesser degree.

In the acceptance by the man, Jesus, He and the Christ became one and shall never part again. For, to have knowledge, is to preclude ignorance, darkness. Once there is Light, there cannot be darkness, for, that which has been seen and known is forever known and seen. See?

Once there is Light, there cannot be darkness, for, that which has been seen and known is forever known and seen.

December 2

There is nothing that is in your life that you are powerless over. That is an illusion. It is possible that life can bring to you things that are, indeed, a challenge or are, indeed, something of sadness or of limitation, and these things can impact the temple in which you dwell to a point.

Once you cross the threshold of being one with yourself – in other words, not that inner self and the outer self, but the one Self with a capital S – then, you control who and what you are and what experiences you have.

But, in the wisdom of your oneness, you recognize the right of others to choose. So, you do not go about putting a color on this one and another color on that one, and changing their lives because, once you have that oneness, you can also see and, in the seeing, comes the realization that they are not alone. They are not helpless. They are where they are because this is something that will contribute to them. Maybe not in this lifetime, or in the next, or in twenty lifetimes, but it will contribute to them once they release it and see it for what it is and ask for something better.

Once you cross the threshold of being one with yourSelf, you control who you are and what experiences you have.

December 3

Abundance is like a great storehouse within you, likened unto a granary filled to overflowing. At the top of this great granary is the opening unto which more grain can be given. At the bottom is that portal from which grain can be withdrawn. If you, as the keeper of this internal granary, are walking through the lands of your life and you see those whom are hungered and you open the doors of the granary and let the grain come forth to nourish their need, in the upper chamber of same our Father shall add more. Greater than that taken from below shall He giveth from above, so that the willing worker will find, joyfully, self hard-pressed to give away the greater sum. It is our Father's Word and His Law, not ours. It is through the Master's works that this has been shown to you. The more He gave, the greater were the blessings given. He took a few loaves and a few fishes that all might meet their need of hunger. The sum of the fragments of same were scores more than the individual sum of that which He began with. Witness, then, that as truth to what we have given.

If you give, greater is given thee. If you give an hundred, one hundred ten is given you, and much more than this, not to our measure, or to those precise numbers, but to the calculation of your willingness to receive and give. If you believe in an eternal, unlimited nature, that is the river of life and abundance is awaiting to pass through you.

If you believe in an eternal, unlimited nature, that is the river of life and abundance is waiting to pass through you.

December 4

It is not without that you would find that which you seek. It is within you.

If it need be, step away from all else and dwell in the peace and comfort of the beauty of your own uniqueness, and dwell in this with Father and each other who believe. And find the peace to know that what you are is as the Christ ... the eternal spirits, children of God who have chosen to journey into the Earth, who have chosen to endure and to pass through those things that are present in the Earth. No matter how you would see these things or judge them, they are simply of the Earth. They are not a part of you unless you hold them to yourself.

Revisit that often. It is what you hold to yourself that becomes a part of you.

It is not without that you would find that which you seek. It is within you.

December 5

What is it that you claim when you claim oneness with the Christ? You do not project a light outwards to some distant point, some star grouping or nebula, or even any of the polestars or such. It is the brightest star of all … It is that which lies within you.

The difficulty that causes some to stumble over this at times is the feeling of going out and seeking and movement.

Here is the clarity of that point: The spirit within you is not bound by your earthly expression's perimeters or definitions. Your spirit does not fit within the physical body in which you are now dwelling. That is its focal point, but your spirit dwells, ever, in a state of oneness with the Spirit of Father.

It is the Spirit of Father that shineth that finger of light that creates the uniqueness of you. It is your love of Father that reflects this back to Father and the expansion of this, to be complete and one with the spirit of Father and the Christ. It is this state of being, this power of acceptance and intent, that is the Christ Spirit within you.

Your spirit does not fit within your physical body. That is its focal point, but your spirit dwells with the Spirit of Father.

December 6

When an entity departs from the Earth plane, obviously they are no longer interested in moving along a singular linear movement.

Yet, so accustomed to this straight-line concept of time or existence are they that, often, many entities will dwell in a state between realms, so to say, between levels of expression, for a time. While they are in this state of time, they are still consciously associating themselves with the idea of progression along a straight line. Hence, it can be stated that a certain entity can be anticipated to be in a state such as this restful one for a measure of Earth years, until such a time as they may be stimulated or receptive to stimulation on the part of those good souls who care for them. And a note here: There are always those souls at hand around those who are in a state of rest or rebalance, to protect, to nurture, and to be ready, should there be the request for further growth.

There are always those souls around those who are in a state of rebalance, to protect and to nurture.

December 7

Man is now at a point of an intent to rid himself of the influences which cause him hardship or disharmony, you see. Dwelling as a being (you would call yourselves) in a more dense state began, you must understand, merely as an experiment on the part of several of the groupings of souls that were created by God, you see.

Over the course of time, there has become such an in-depth involvement that too many are continuing to, let us say, orbit the same pathway repeatedly, though there is always progress. This is a spiraling orbit which will reach a point of movement sooner or later to another plane of functioning. See? Your intent, in its purest sense, that you all seek is the peak of that spiral.

Man is now at a point of an intent to rid himself of the influences which cause him hardship or disharmony.

December 8

Time is multidimensional. Time does not cease simply because you have measured it and called it "past." Hence, a moment of your time may be as an eternity on other realms, and eternity would be, perhaps, just a moment elsewhere. This is experienced often in near-death situations, or wherein entities have been exceedingly physically diseased and find a review of their entire lifetime taking a span of mere moments of time.

In terms of this, then, one should be mindful that some souls are well prepared to return very quickly in terms of your measurement. Other souls may not find purposeful need to return quickly but may function, then, on other planes. Still other souls may require some period of balancing before they can accept the fact that they have not died within their bodies. (Such cases can be extremely difficult.)

A moment of your time may be an eternity on other realms, and eternity would be, perhaps, just a moment elsewhere.

December 9

No suffering is required by God. Suffering is imposed by the soul, itself, and the conscious minds involved. If God were such as to punish thee for each wrong doing, He would be quite busy, would He not? He would be alternating moment to moment from sadness to joy and joy to sadness.

There is this as a benefit from such suffering: Suffering brings about, seemingly, the reduction of the conscious mind to a level wherein it begins to be receptive to its own eternal nature. It is an odd and curious point, when viewed from our levels, that the physical-mental body often needs to be reduced to its lowest point in order to accept themselves as a part of God. So, to that extent, suffering seems to be beneficial … though, we are in a quandary as to why one does not simply accept this at the onset and have a joyful existence, as God intended thee.

How to understand one's shortcomings and to balance karmically with past experiences requires only that one fully accept and understand at all levels of mind that this has been an experience in the past, and that this experience has been to teach, to guide, and to bring forth the growth of love. Once this is done there is no longer any need for suffering or that karmic involvement. Do you see?

Suffering brings the reduction of the conscious mind to a level where it begins to be receptive to its own eternal nature.

December 10

The highest acceptance of God is just that ... acceptance of God without any reservations.

If any one of you in your gathering at this point were to truly accept God – not on your terms but as God exists, this very moment, in, about, and throughout eternity – with thee, then, this is the achievement of the highest plane, for, thee would realize that your existence on the Earth plane and elsewhere is through your own wish to do so. As this is clearer and clearer, you approach that point which is referred to as Heaven, you see.

Heaven is a state of awareness. It is to exist and know that you exist. It is to be and know that you are. It is that which is "I am I." It is eternal.

Heaven is a state of awareness ... to exist and know that you exist, to be and know that you are. It is that which is "I am I."

December 11

Often, the mental body that you exist as in the physical plane, where your body-physical exists, becomes so confused by the mass-thought that it begins to believe that it must age and must have disease, and must be sad and morose at times. Then, a reviewing of past lifetimes can prove to one that this is just an experience for you.

Past lifetimes can often fragmentarily affect your physical body and your mental mind in your present existence. A case in point ... an entity who might have some serious crippling disease for which your medical doctors find no explainable cause, perhaps the right hand or arm. In searching through past records, this entity might find that with their right hand they did smite a brother and strike them dead. This, at the subconscious level, is considered an act of error, so, the conscious mind, receiving some impulses unknowingly, is guided by the subconscious and causes the right arm not to be capable of repeating this error. (This is a rather dramatic case.)

All of your dis-ease in the physical plane begins at the mental level. Do you see? There is no disease other than that created by the mind.

There is no disease other than that created by the mind.

December 12

Existence is often misinterpreted ...

Every leaf on a tree is a part of that tree. Is it not? Without the tree it does not exist. Hence, if you were leaves upon a tree, you would look at yourselves as individuals, which you are. When viewed from a distance, you are a tree.

Your experience on the physical plane is as a leaf on that tree. Your soul is the entire tree, or, the sum of the experiences. The tree grows in a meadow. Upon this meadow are several trees. These trees are called a forest. This forest, then, is called a group of souls. This, then, when viewed from a distance might be seen, not as a forest, but, rather, as a form or geographic shape of a continent ... and so on, you see, until we find that one is viewing God.

But, without that leaf on that single tree, that forest is not complete. It is lacking.

There is a need for you to exist, for, God created each of our souls for the purpose of companionship, in a manner of speaking. For, one who has no limit to love, kindness, compassion, must share ... must exist, not as a singular being, for, there is no interaction in singularity. There is interaction and compassion and all expressions when there is multiplicity of existence.

There is a need for you to exist, for, God created each of our souls for the purpose of companionship.

December 13

The life force which is that called the animal is, generally speaking, attached to those souls with whom it exists. Therefore, if one has an animal as a domesticated pet and exudes kindnesses and love towards this life force, this gives a very individualistic character to that life force, helping that life force to shape itself into a more definable portion. That life force, then, will follow the physical or soul's life force usually on its journey throughout times, as you call it. To that extent it is capable of reentering nearly any animal form that is available to that soul in future incarnations.

Therefore, an entity who has had an animal called a dog in past life who was very much loved, may find that, strangely, a bird may be found having the same characteristics to that soul in future life. This can also occur within the same lifetime. For an entity to have one animal at early years, to have it demise, that life force exists very near to that entity and, if the opportunity presents itself, it will reenter, as permitted, to join that soul in its continued journey. This can occur repeatedly during any individual's lifetime. Eventually, an animal spirit (as it's called) can assume much the individualistic characteristics similar to a soul through that love and that creative giving, which is from its master. This is a somewhat complex pattern but, to some extent, the soul here, itself, is creating, to a large degree, through the love.

The life force which is that called the animal is, generally speaking, attached to those souls with whom it exists.

December 14

Predestination has the involvement of the soul's pattern or plan. You enter the Earth plane with the understanding that the physical body will have, as its influences and effects, the sum total of mankind's mass-thought, as society views it at that point ... the effect of the thoughts of the entities called your parents or guardians or what have you, the understanding that certain souls who are viewed and understood at that time to be in existence with you.

You will understand and see all these opportunities. To that extent, you are predestined, but not without your choice. It is your free choice here, you see, to choose that destiny.

There is a soul's destiny here that is often overlooked. Each soul plans and has, as its destiny, an understanding of and a return to that point of total awareness as a part of God, yet retaining its individual God-given nature.

Each soul plans and has, as its destiny, an understanding of and a return to that point of total awareness as a part of God.

December 15

In a moment of time, as you measure this, God's thought welled up in a tremendous void of indefinable space and souls suddenly emerged as the creation of a mass, benevolent, joyous thought, exploding into existence in such a way that is inconceivable to your minds as they dwell at that point of your plane. To that extent, then, in all directions, in all places, all corners of that which is known to exist, did souls enter existence. These are you we are speaking of ... each of you. Billions of years, as you would measure them, have you existed.

A soul cannot die. All souls, in the terms which you define this, were created in this moment ... and this moment, in a manner of speaking, is your present now.

In a moment of time, God's thought welled up and souls emerged. All souls were created in this moment.

December 16

Karmic patterns are merely the soul's pattern of development. Karma is a gift, in a manner of speaking. It allows you to right those things, which are out of balance. Not to atone for wrongs or sufferings, but to bring balance within self through understanding and experience. If you have wronged a brother in a past lifetime, it does not mean that, in order to balance with that throughout eternity, you must, accordingly, be wronged. For, it is not the deed, not the word, but the thought behind this that needs the understanding.

In this instance, where was thine compassion for this entity? It was dormant. Hence, your lesson, then, would be the need to develop a higher understanding of compassion. So, in your next lifetime, you may choose to come back into a body which will probably choose a pathway of healing or service, such as a priestly man or priestly woman, one who would dedicate and have compassion to all levels. Do you see? Another might choose to come back as an extremely wealthy man and, then, find that wealth will not bring about that which is joyous in his life. Realizing this, he understands that, through compassion and kindness, must he atone, in a very loose use of that term, for the past experience.

Karma is a gift ... not to atone for wrongs or sufferings, but to bring balance to self through understanding and experience.

December 17

It is not an idle purpose that you exist on your Earth plane. It is extremely important. It is an honor, a privilege and a joy, to have an opportunity to assist other souls ... including your self. You exist as you believe you exist, for, thou art a creator, a co-creator with God. That which you exist as is that which benefits our soul's purpose and the sum total of inter-active purpose with other souls. So, therefore, this is of much importance.

Because a man thinketh himself well and he is well is that not good? If a man thinketh ill of himself and becomes ill, is that not, on your terms, bad?

So, a man, then, as a physical being, learns to balance his mental body, his spiritual, and physical body, that it can relate to all these experiences and have growth, that he learns to control his creative power, that he learns to be a contributor towards God, his brethren, and life, itself.

It is not an idle purpose that you exist on your Earth plane. It is extremely important. It is an honor, a privilege.

December 18

Using hypnosis to regress a person to the state between lives to allow for the discovery of or the goals or objectives can be done, providing it does not interfere with that soul's original choice and that soul's free will at the higher self level. It does not mean, necessarily, that an inquisitive mental body can knock upon the door of eternal knowledge and have it opened unto him, when such knowledge might damage or injure their purpose. This is why some entities achieve more satisfying results (to their thinking).

Nothing of value can be lost, to the extent that one retains, not the specifics, perhaps, but the thoughts behind them. An example here might be that, if one is wealthy in this lifetime and has had all that this plane can give beneficially in a physical sense, does not necessarily mean that that soul will recall that wealth but will recall the effect of that wealth upon their mental, spiritual body. If they deal with that wealth wisely and in a charitable or spiritual way, then, this is what they will recall. They will not lose anything, but they will not recall, necessarily, it in the same context.

In terms of regression, you cannot lose that which is your experiences. These are permanent. You can better understand them. Regression, to understand and to realize that it is merely a past experience, can have untold benefit to them in their present lifetime.

Regressing a person does not necessarily mean the door will be opened, when the knowledge might damage their purpose.

December 19

Love is as its first letter. It is as one would extend an arm to embrace. It is as one would extend their thought, their encouragement, that upon which you can rest or rise, that which looks to the potential within and sees not that which is the limitation, that which has been claimed because there is not knowledge of claiming it not.

Love is not an expression which is symbolized, enacted, or brought into creative force through physical bodies. Love is the willingness to stand at a distance and hold good intentions for another while they may know not you are so doing. Love is the willingness to release those who have wronged thee, that they might find their own righteousness. Love is the power through which great wondrous works can be accomplished. Love and compassion are inseparable.

Love and compassion are inseparable.

December 20

It is well for you to remember, dear friend, that, of all the souls in the kingdom of our Father, not one is greater or lesser in His sight or in His love. And, while there are those who have risen to great heights of spiritual acceptance of their oneness with Him, neither shall these, those who have illuminated the path, the way, ever forget one soul left behind.

Therefore, do we find of this nature, this spiritual truth, that the soul who was expressed as the counterpoint to the Master, the man called Jesus, then called Mary, is, equally so, at the side of the Master in joyous service and in the dedication of Her heart, Her spirit, as can be found in each soul to those whom would seek and wish to know the way.

We urge you to remember that it is not your conditioning, your certain preference in terms of the theosophy, that can ever "make one worthy" but, rather, it is what is in the heart, not that that cometh from the mouth, that is of eternal import and truth.

Know your heart to be ever in harmony with the spiritual forces that are seeking to make the way passable for the illumination of the Christ Spirit in the Earth, once again. It is of this work, this activity, that we find it given here that the appearances of Mary are becoming more frequent and widespread, even as we speak.

It is what is in the heart, not that that cometh from the mouth, that is of eternal import and truth.

December 21

So would it not be that Mary with the Master, the Christ, as one harmonious union ... that these would come to the Earth and that She, as the bearer of His heart, of His love, of His long-suffering, and of His truth, might seek to cause those who would be willing to hear and know to release their doubt, their fear? To fast, not from this or that food, but from errant thought? To pray and meditate, that they would bring joy and freedom into their lives, not bondage? That they would know the greatest temple of all is within each individual, and that no church is greater than the Earth, itself, for God is not confined in a simple chamber, but is within all.

If you seek, then, religion, do so with joy and with an attitude of freedom, but not as a mandatory pre-requisite to knowing and seeing Mary, twin to the Christ. For She is already in your heart and spirit as surely as you hear these words. That same spirit, a spark of the One Light, glows within you, even now. If you should see Her, it is because She intends it to be so because She might wish to lift a burden, to remove a veil, or, She may wish that your heart may join the river of light growing each day in honor to the man called Jesus. As the flow of God's spirit through each new entity joining in that intent and ideal grows, so is the time hastened to the coming of the Light and the time of potential paradise on Earth.

A spark of the One Light, glows within you, even now.

December 22

The greater one becomes unburdened, unlimited and free in their spiritual acceptance, the more unlimited are they in their potential of movement. Therefore, it is with utter ease that Mary may move into and out of the Earth or, by thrusting a finger of Her thought forth into the Earth, project Herself to wherever She would will. And, as the Master stands by Her side, the knowledge is clear: The time is upon the Earth of unfoldment, of enlightenment, that those things of old ... thoughts, attitudes and such ... must be lain aside as one removes old garments to receive the new. Old thoughts cast off for bright new enlightening ones, healthful and at ease.

We believe this to be the beginning of this time of change, and we believe that others will see and hear and know more and more truth, and that other sightings, other appearances, other messengers, will grow in their frequency, their clarity, and their profoundness. You have the message already within you. The call is from the needy, not the faithful. The faithful are already one with God and it is their light and their faith which can contribute to the intent of Mary and others ... many, many others.

Mary may, by thrusting a finger of Her thought forth into the Earth, project Herself to wherever She would will.

December 23

We have, in essence, paralleled footsteps from the same body. Whereas one would walk with a foot on one side and the other on the other side of a line called consciousness, it was, in the ultimate, the same form which took the steps. Complete. See? That, as Mary suffered, Jesus provided strength and, as Jesus was enhungered, Mary provided nourishment. When Joseph spoke truth and was guided by God that he should be recognized in the lands of the Egyptians, that guidance was through Mary. Where Joshua was possessed of the will of God, it was the completeness of his interaction with the expression of himself called Mary that enabled his wisdom and power to prevail over the forces of illusion. Do you see? Mary, then, walks not behind Jesus, not in his shadow, but at his side.

The simple action of walking exemplifies the cooperative coexistence of companion souls, twin souls, soul mates. The next time you take a step, the next time you speak, ask, was it the word, the will, the demonstrative power of prayer, or was it that which nourishes the soul, heals with the sustenance of God, brings forth support and encouragement, elucidates truth and faith? In other words, had ye spoken through the principle of Jesus or through the principle of Mary, and, in the final aspect of that, is it of import to know which, or, to simply know that these are the examples that ye might follow and the memories which ye might invoke, that, as there is the need, ye would know of it and summon it unto that task.

Mary, Jesus ... examples ye might follow, memories ye might invoke, as there is the need, and summon forth unto that task.

December 24

Each Christ Mass, hold the thought that, at the instant of unification of body, mind, and spirit unto this, the man called Jesus, there was fashioned within each of you this same seed. Then, when you next celebrate His mass, celebrate that mass within, and try each day of Earth consciousness to nourish it just a bit. Give it thy gifts of love, of faith, of charity, forgiveness, compassion, all of those aspects as ye know are His.

So as ye do, know, ever, that thou art one step closer unto that moment when the very finger of God shall pierce through the darkness of those realms of Earth to light upon *thee*, to proclaim to all:

"This is my Child of whom I am most pleased."

In the spirit of the Christ, we here, who are most humble to be with thee, proclaim to you that this is what shall be: Each of you shall have your moment as the Christ. Each of you shall be born into that of the simplicity of the Earth, shall be raised up under the care and guidance of loving souls, and shall use each of those gifts given by loving entities in these realms, whereupon, there shall emerge the jewel of your soul, which is the promise of God unto thee ... the Christ. And, in that moment whereupon there must be the decision to cling to the flesh or to cleave from it that jewel, ye shall know the answer to all that ye seek, and there shall be remembered, then, not only this mass, but that moment when you were united with the Christ.

Thee ... "This is my Child of whom I am most pleased."

December 25

We greet you joyously at this time so hallowed as that which is the eternal grace and salvation of all time. The symbol of the Christ Mass is the symbol of opportunity given to all forces in all realms. As there is, from a tiny seed of expectation of grandeur, let this Christmas be as that seed within self, that it shall have the expectation of the highest grandeur that you can conceive; and that, as the seed grows and draws its nourishment from the eternal God, and its branches reach beyond to caress and to give love and sharing to all, think in your heart that, without the harmonious existence of all the forces, the grandeur and vision of that seed might never be.

Then, nourish the visions of thy brethren. Be that which supports them and, truly, give them love. Let this be, now, the beginning of a dawning within self, that thine eyes shall behold that which is of glory in each soul and shall see not that which in past disturbed thee.

Wait until the sun has set for the evening and step out and become at one with the vastness of God, lift your head to the heavens and perceive the jewels which God has spread across His robe, see the eternal light which comes from every one and perceive the beauty and immensity of this garment, and know – at that instant – that it was created just for thee, that it was and is a protective garb to nurture thee, the seed of God, with grand and glorious expectations. Let the Christ be born, then, within.

———

Let the Christ be born, then, within.

December 26

The celebration of the Christ Spirit is a daily one on behalf of those who hold the Master as their brother. Yet, even so, does this daily celebration and desire to move into greater oneness with Him accumulate. It does so as a crescendo of faith, of hope, of service. And that crescendo comes into its full manifestation on the day you call the Christ Mass.

As you have of recent times visited this ceremony, this celebration, it is our collective prayer here, in those who dwell beyond the Earth, that as your journey leads you on into the next Earth year measure, you would be inspired by this Christ Mass to look, to ask – not aloud, not in word, but in spirit – of each whom you meet, "Is the Christ within you awakened?" Look into their eyes as you say this in your spirit, in your mind, in your heart, and see if a light appears, even if ever so briefly. And, when it does, give thanks and claim it, knowing that the Christ within you has called forth and made a bond, a connection of light, with a brother or sister in the journey called life.

Build within yourselves a temple, a temple which has no walls, which needs no ceiling, a temple which is open and alive. And whatsoe'er ye might name this, or how ye might build it, look for Him there, and ye will find Him. That is our prayer for you, one and all, from we, one and all. May the Christ Mass live on in each day in your hearts, minds, and spirits. We bless you.

Build within yourselves a temple … no walls, no ceiling … open and alive. Look for Him there, and ye will find Him.

December 27

The Spirit called Christ is the eternal essence of the children of God. It is the Light, the presence of Life itself, and it is eternal. It is the source of Truth, it is the reservoir of omnipotent Power and nothing is beyond its potential. In the Earth, so many would have it seem that only the man called Jesus bears this gift from God and, yet, in His own words and teachings did He say different than this.

How could our Master say to you, to all of us, that *All these things and greater shall ye do* if He did not know that that within Him is also within all others? For, it is, as he demonstrated, this Christ Spirit which doeth the work.

The Spirit called Christ is the eternal essence of the children of God. It is the presence of Life itself, eternal, omnipotent.

December 28

We would express again to thee, just briefly, the importance of understanding that reincarnation is a fact. Each of you in existence, there at this time, has existed before this time in other bodies or in other life forms. We do not see any soul among thy gathering who has not had experiences on one plane or another in past. To deny this heritage, this grand heritage of self, is much the same as denying one's own abilities towards the enjoyment of, let us say, music or colors, or paintings, or works of art, or constructions of mind and body. It is a part of thee.

The sooner that your present society begins the greater acceptance of this, the more rapidly shall be your blessings. For, through the denial of self as an eternal, evolving being, there is much of the denial of one's own ability to control one's present life. Reminding you, you have not a need for dis-ease. This is accepted by some part of your mind, else it would not exist.

Through the denial of self as an eternal, evolving being, there is the denial of one's own ability to control one's present life.

December 29

It is interesting, is it not, dear friends, to attend a symphony, where all involved, each participant, has prepared themselves, that they are ready to the utmost of their being to contribute their part as a single voice, a single instrument, in the orchestra or the choir. Then, as you prepare yourself to hear this, if you are in the audience, you have an attitude of anticipation. So, we have the producers, the choir or the orchestra who has carefully and lovingly prepared themselves and their instruments and you, who have come to attend, anticipating something of wonder. You, as well, have prepared yourselves in many fine ways. You are all there, now, and you await the conductor.

Think about it, for, this is the current state of the Earth.

Each of you is as the conductor. Are you prepared, as though you are one voice, one instrument, or do you wish to be an observer? In either case, know who you are, where you are, what you are, and do the best that you can to bring this to a wondrous presentation. The Earth is much like an eager listener. Who shall be the conductor? If everyone believes that they are of such responsibility, would the care and the beauty with which the presentation is given not be wondrous? And, if that symphonic intent is agreed upon, as an attitude of love and compassion, of peace, of joy, will the Earth, then, not find this as something wondrous to follow? You are not just the result. You are a part of the creation *and* the result.

You are not just the result. You are a part of the creation *and* the result.

December 30

No matter what comes, what knocks upon thy door, answer it with faith and peace. The Father's love for thee has no barriers, no limitations.

It is good for you, then, in these current times to find that condition of mind, of spirit, of emotion that can embrace the peace of God, which has been given thee, which is being offered.

Pause to look, to see, to hear, to know and, when there is question or doubt, ask and it will be given.

Above all, keep your faith to the forefront in all matters, and this will ever provide you with the endurance you are seeking, and joyfully so.

Above all, keep your faith to the forefront in all matters, and this will provide you with the endurance you are seeking.

December 31

Let the light of the hopefulness of the Christ Mass be greater than ever before.

This is the threshold of the beginning. At its terminus, He will enter. Celebrate, and be free of doubt and fear.

Claim hope, and it will be given to thee.

Be free of doubt and fear. Claim hope, and it will be given to thee.

We depart at this time, then, giving thanks to all those beloved entities who have gathered here in service to those brethren on the Earth plane.

We ask that that spirit which binds all entities into oneness be awakened, that that of the Master's light as a pathway, as a patterning, can be understood. We ask, as well, that each soul who reads these words has the greater joy, as those from this unseen world would reach out at this moment to touch the brow and bless each one.

Let there be, too, among these children of the Master's flock, that of His healing light and knowledge, that, within them each is awakened that spark, that kindle of light, which is of the Master, that those things which are called dis-ease . . . Please, we ask at this time, let them be released as that soul allows them to be released. This we ask in His name.

God be with thee, then, one and all.
Fare thee well.

Lama Sing

Books by Al Miner & Lama Sing ...

The Chosen: *Back Story to the Essene Legacy*
The Promise: *Book I of The Essene Legacy*
The Awakening: *Book II of The Essene Legacy*
The Path: *Book III of The Essene Legacy*

In Realms Beyond: *Book I of The Peter Chronicles*
In Realms Beyond: *Study Guide*
Awakening Hope: *Book II of The Peter Chronicles*

Death, Dying, and Beyond: *How to Prepare for The Journey* Vol I
The Sea of Faces: *How to Prepare for The Journey* Vol II

Jesus: *Book I*
Jesus: *Book II*

The Course in Mastery

When Comes the Call

Seed Thoughts

For a comprehensive list of reading transcripts available, visit the Lama Sing library at www.lamasing.net

About Al Miner

A chance hypnosis session in 1973 began Al's tenure as the channel for Lama Sing. Since then, nearly 10,000 readings have been given in a trance state answering technical and personal questions on such topics as science, health and disease, history, geophysics, spirituality, philosophy, metaphysics, past and future times, and much more. The validity of the information has been substantiated and documented by research institutions and individuals. Those receiving personal readings continue to refer others to Al's work based on the accuracy and integrity of the information in their readings. In 1984, St. Johns University awarded Al an honorary doctoral degree in parapsychology.

Al conducts a variety of field research projects, as well as occasional workshops and lectures. He occasionally accepts requests for personal readings, but is mostly devoting his remaining time to works intended to be good for all. Much of his current research is dedicated to the concept that the best of all guidance is that which comes from within.

Al lives with his wife in the mountains of Western North Carolina.

Made in the USA
Middletown, DE
05 January 2022

57787336R00209